Cutting CURVES from STRAIGHT PIECES

Debbie Bowles

American Quilter's Society

P. O. Box 3290 • Paducah, KY 42002-3290
www.AQSquilt.com

Located in Paducah, Kentucky, the American Quilter's Society (AQS) is dedicated to promoting the accomplishments of today's quilters. Through its publications and events, AQS strives to honor today's quilt-makers and their work and to inspire future creativity and innovation in quiltmaking.

EDITOR: BARBARA SMITH
GRAPHIC DESIGN: LYNDA SMITH
COVER DESIGN: MICHAEL BUCKINGHAM
PHOTOGRAPHY: CHARLES R. LYNCH

Library of Congress Cataloging-in-Publication Data
Bowles, Debbie
    Cutting curves from straight pieces / Debbie Bowles
        p. cm.
    Includes index.
        ISBN 1-57432-757-7
        1. Quilting--Patterns. 2. Patchwork--Patterns. I. Title.
TT835 .B6355 2000
    746.46'041--dc21   00-12253

Additional copies of this book may be ordered from the American Quilter's Society, PO Box 3290, Paducah, KY 42002-3290, or online at: www.AQSquilt.com.

Dedication

To
Rick,
   Ryan,
      and
         Kyle
            who always
               celebrated
               my victories
            and
         never
      complained
   when all the
bent pieces
   began to
      take over.

Acknowledgments

This book couldn't have become a finished project without help from all the following people. Thanks to...

Sue Herzberg at Country Needleworks in Eagan, Minnesota, for all her support, advice, and teaching space.

Pat Eastlund, Cheryl Forsythe, Beverly Dorsey, and Sandra Tundel for their commitment, enthusiasm, and sense of humor as they tested, created, and did their own curved piecing.

Jan Loomer and Kay Smith for letting me join the fun of their new venture.

All of the students and friends who allowed their quilts to be included in this book.

Brenda Leino at Plaid Farm Quilting, who machine quilted some of these projects and always came up with great ideas.

Barbara Smith at the American Quilter's Society, who had time to answer all my questions.

Princess Mirah Bali Fabrics; Balson-Hercules Group, Ltd.; Hoffman California Fabrics; Omnigrid, Inc; and Perfect Cotton for generously providing some of the supplies that were used in some projects.

Contents

Introduction

Frequently, I am asked how I thought of cutting curves from straight pieces. It didn't come to me in the middle of the night or anything wonderfully dramatic like that. I was trying to piece a two-color spiral, similar to Snail's Trail, from single pieces of fabric. I never did get the spiral to work, but the rejected strips with the curved seams appeared to offer quick, easy, fun quilts with unexpected results.

There are three types of curves used in the projects. In the three lessons, which begin on page 14, you will find complete instructions for creating the single curve, multiple curves, and arcs and half circles. The directions are written so the practice pieces can be made into an attractive wallhanging.

Rather than just reading about the practice pieces, please try them. The lessons contain technical information that is not repeated in the projects, and you will learn more easily and more completely by practicing. With these techniques, you will quickly become an "expert" in curved cutting and piecing and will be ready for all the projects.

In each project, you will find step-by-step illustrated instructions. Ideal measurements are given at various times during quilt construction. These can be used as guides for adding pieces, such as borders. The border and other measurements given are exact, but every quilter sews a little differently. So, before cutting your pieces to length, you may want to measure your quilt and compare it to the ideal measurements. If they differ by more than ⅛", which can be eased, you have the choice of taking in or letting out some of the quilt seams or changing the cut lengths of the pieces to match the actual quilt measurements. Taking a little time to measure your quilt, square up corners, and straighten raw edges at each stage of the assembly will make all the pieces go together easily.

I hope you have great fun creating curves. The possibilities for curved segments are far ranging. There are many still waiting for discovery, so take a chance and cut some curves!

Possibilities

The possibilities for curved pieces are unlimited. Books with traditional block collections are great resources. They are filled with quilt blocks just waiting to be curved. A new block with a traditional base is there for you to discover.

Here are some ideas to get you started:

Two strips of contrasting fabric…

can become this curved section.

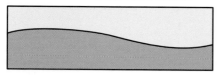

Three sewn strips can become…

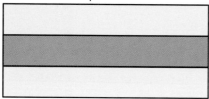

this double curved section.

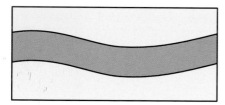

A pieced curve layered with an unpieced strip…

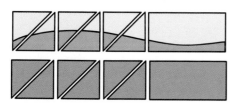

can make interesting half-square units.

Substitute curved pieces for parts of a traditional block:

Churn Dash

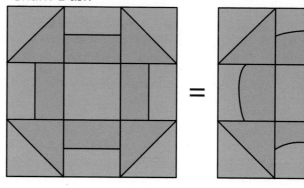

Spirit of St. Louis

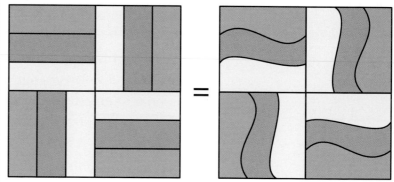

Chain and Hourglass

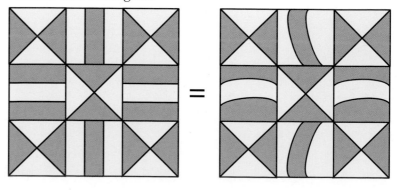

Cutting Curves from Straight Pieces – Debbie Bowles

Possibilities

Many of the curved pieces in these quilts can also make interesting borders and sashing. Keep in mind that, with many of the pieces, you create an identical shape in reversed fabrics. Remember also that most of them have edges that are not on the straight of grain, so they will benefit from a final border cut on the grain.

Rail Fence variation

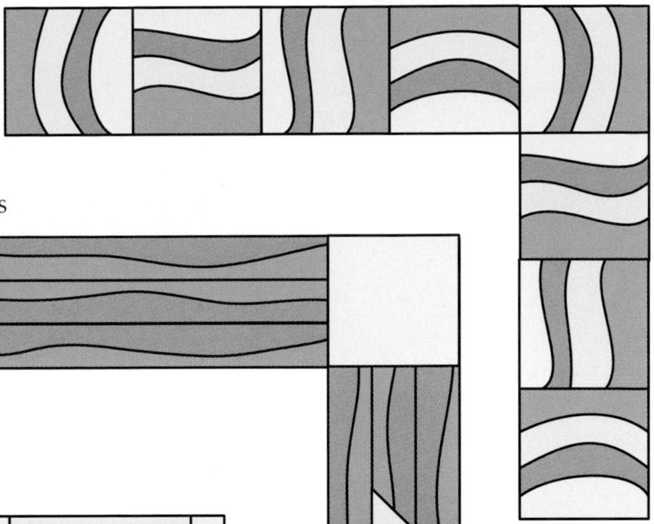

Curves and Stars

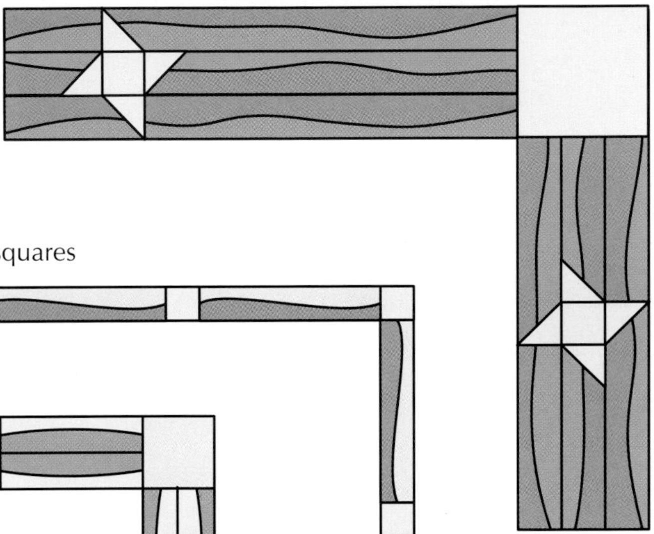

Curved strips with squares

Arc segments with squares

Alternating colors

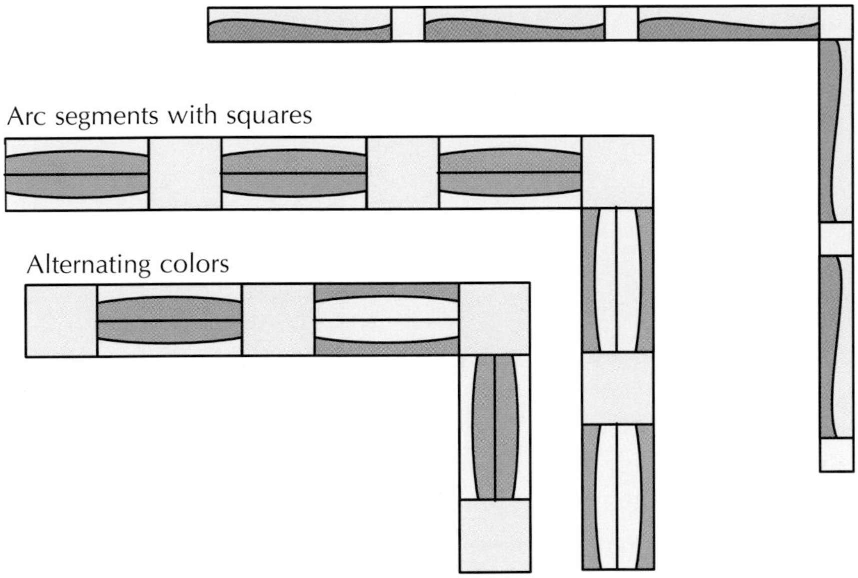

Half-circles

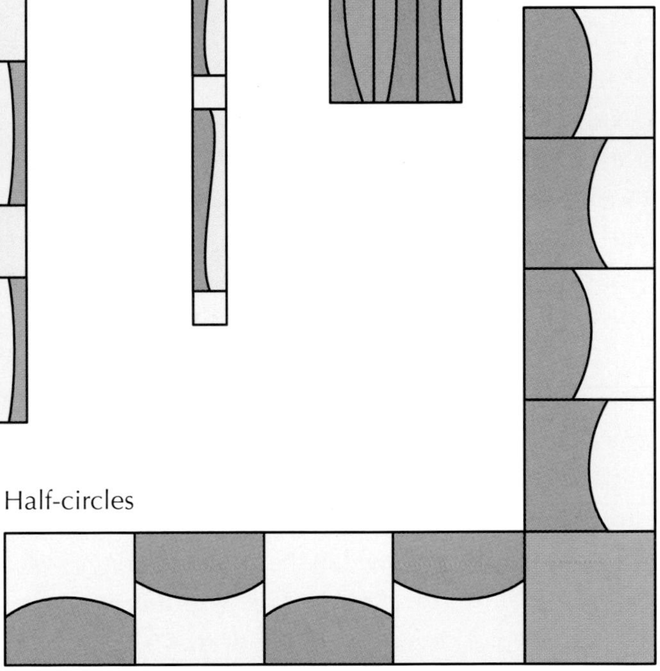

Circles

Alternating colors

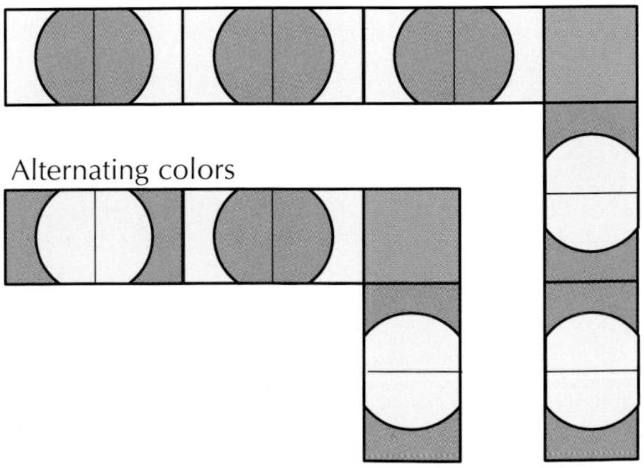

Checkerboard

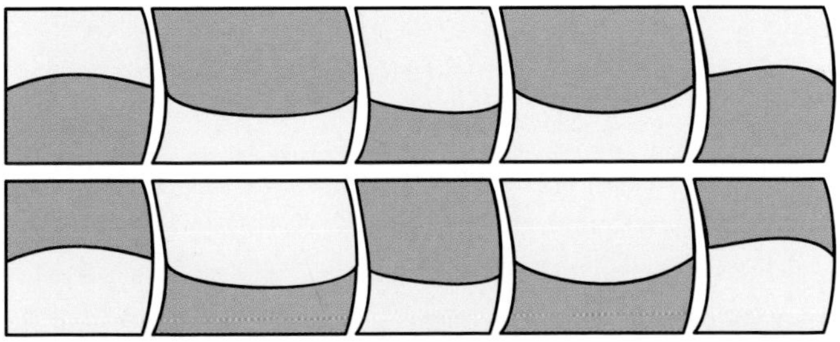

Cutting Curves from Straight Pieces – Debbie Bowles

Quiltmaking Tips

This book is not intended to teach you the basics of quiltmaking. There are many fine publications available to do that. However, the following information is a collection of skills and tips that may help you with some of the projects.

Supplies

Rotary cutting mat, at least 17" x 22".
Rotary cutter with sharp blade.
Acrylic ruler for rotary cutting, size 6" x 24".
Square acrylic rulers or templates, 6½" and 12½",
   for squaring blocks in some projects.
Sewing machine and basic sewing supplies
Marking pencil
Sense of adventure

Vertical design surface

A vertical design surface is helpful for all quilt projects. It allows you to view your work straight-on rather than looking down on it. You can see the big picture of how the elements of your project are working together. If you have the space for a permanent design surface, consider a large piece of cardboard or styrofoam covered with flannel, felt, or batting attached to the wall. The fibers will grab the fabric pieces and hold them in place without pins, allowing you to move the pieces around quickly when trying out designs. For a temporary design surface, tack flannel or batting to the molding on a large window. Let the flannel hang down over the window. If you have a large window with drapes, pin the flannel or batting to the drapes.

Fabric selection

With curved pieces, you must use high-contrast color or value (light and dark) or the curve will be lost. You can control the appearance of your quilt by the choice of fabric, the cut of the curve, and the placement of the block or strip. The options are enormous. These curves hold the possibility of exciting "accidents" that are impossible to predict.

Quarter-Square Triangles

For efficiency in making pieced quilts with quarter-square triangles (see LETTING LOOSE, page 56), try the following chain-sewing method of stacking, stitching, and pressing.

○ Arrange the quarter-square triangles in stacks for sewing based on color selection.

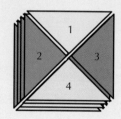

○ Place triangle 1 on top of triangle 2, right sides together, and 3 on top of 4, right sides together.

Sew the first pair of triangles and, without lifting the needle or cutting the threads, sew the next pair. Continue adding pairs of triangles to the chain.

Cutting Curves from Straight Pieces – Debbie Bowles

○ Take the entire chain of triangles to the ironing board. Open the triangle pairs and press the seam allowances as directed by the arrows in the figure. Leave the chains between the half-squares that will be sewn together, but clip the chains between the "squares."

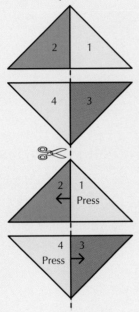

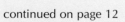

○ Place half-square 3–4 on top of half-square 1–2 and sew. Chain sew all the half-squares together. Press the seam allowances in either direction.

continued on page 12

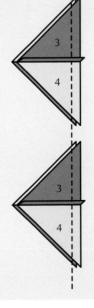

If you like fabric motifs to run in the same direction, you should probably avoid directional fabrics. The curved strips and segments are frequently turned in opposite directions when sewn together. It really becomes a personal issue with no right or wrong answer. Simply choose what looks good to you. If you decide to use a directional fabric, think about where the segments will be placed and rotate half the strips or segments before cutting the curves.

Batting

There are many battings for the quilter to choose from, and many quilters have personal favorites. How you will use your quilt, how you plan to quilt it, and what appeals to your eye all affect which batting you choose for each project.

Sewing and pressing

All seam allowances are ¼" wide unless otherwise noted, and the project directions provide information for pressing seam allowances. Pressing is important for matching curved seams effectively. Always trim selvages from fabric. Some selvages are so tightly woven that the fabric will not lie flat until they are removed.

The outside edges of curved segments are not on the true straight grain and may be stretched if handled carelessly. If your cut segments do not join well, pin them before stitching.

Borders

You are quite sure that everything was properly pieced, but when you measure the quilt top before cutting the borders, it is not quite the measurement given in the project. Sound familiar? The tape measure you are using to measure the quilt top is probably not identical to the ruler you used for the cutting. Even a slight difference will add up when it is time to measure 80" to 100". Always measure the quilt top before cutting the borders to size and use the same tape measure for all border measuring.

Cutting Curves from Straight Pieces – Debbie Bowles

Quiltmaking Tips

The quilt top should always be measured through the middle in both directions. I measure all of the edges also. I want to know in advance if I need to do any easing or if a seam has pulled apart somewhere.

Frequently, quilters will find that the sides of their quilts are longer than the middle. The first thing I have students check is the top border seam. It may have pulled apart just slightly during the "admiration" stage of quilting, when you are showing it to friends. We want everyone to get a full view of our project, so we hold it by the top border. To prevent distortion, place your completed quilt top on batting and keep it there until you are ready to quilt it. It will cling to the batting, allowing you to hold the batting, not the top edge of the quilt top, when displaying it. All the weight and drag will be on the batting, not your perfectly pieced quilt top. This becomes especially important if the quilt top has curved segments in the borders.

Cut matching borders two at a time. This assures that they will be the same size and the quilt will be even. If you are piecing border strips, press the seam allowances open.

To attach borders, find the middle of the border strip and the middle of the quilt top edge. Match these centers and pin generously, moving toward the outside edges. If the border is long, divide the quilt top and border segments into quarters and match the quarters. Cut the borders to the proper measurement, then fit the quilt top to the border. Seam allowances are usually pressed toward the borders. Any exceptions will be noted in the instructions.

Backing

The backing yardage for these projects allows for at least 2" around all sides of the quilt top. For projects that are 40"–45" square, the amount of backing becomes quite large because you must have enough for two panels even though the project is just a little wider than one width of the fabric. Rather than joining two

Quarter-Square Triangles continued.

❍ Trim the pieced quarter-squares to the appropriate size.

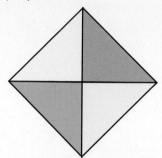

Stitch-and-Flip Triangles

This easy trick is used in the PARADE tablecloth (page 50) and THELMA'S CHOICE wallhanging (page 96).

❍ On the wrong side of the square, mark a diagonal line.

❍ With right sides together, place the square at one end of the strip. Sew on the line.

Cutting Curves from Straight Pieces – Debbie Bowles

○ Flip the corner of the square down, folding it in half along the stitching line. Check to see that the edges are aligned, then press.

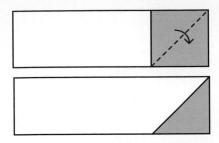

○ Trim off the bottom two triangles, leaving a ¼" seam allowance. The trimmed triangles can be reserved for another project.

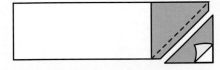

Measuring Borders

○ The quilt top should always be measured through the middle in both directions. I measure all of the edges also. I want to know in advance if I need to do any easing or if a seam has pulled apart somewhere.

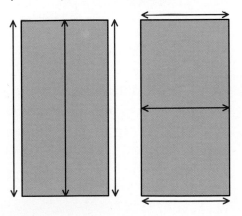

panels, consider making the backing wider by splitting it on the fold and inserting a strip of another fabric large enough to provide the extra inches you need. There is more sewing with this method, but you will have saved some of those fabric dollars for your next quilt.

Quilting

You will find a few words about the quilting of each project. Generally, I begin by stitching in the ditch with monofilament thread on most block or segment seam lines. I add more lines of quilting with cotton, rayon, or metallic thread. I do much of my own quilting and keep it fairly simple because that is the look that appeals to me. Some projects in this book have lovely large spaces that are just calling out for spectacular quilting. I was fortunate to have Brenda Leino, a professional long-arm quilter, working with me. She used many traditional and nontraditional designs in the projects she quilted and used a variety of thread types. All quilts should be squared again after quilting.

Binding

Binding is an important part of the finishing. All the instructions are for double-fold binding. In the patterns, binding strips are usually cut from selvage to selvage. The strips are then sewn end to end with diagonal seams for a smoother look. After sewing the binding strips together, fold and press the sewn strip in half lengthwise, wrong sides together, before sewing it to the quilt.

Quilt labels

Do label your quilts in some way. Generations from now, someone will be happy to know the details of their treasure. I zigzag a quilt label to the backing fabric before layering the quilt. Oftentimes, I use an extra block or cut squares of excess fabric used in the quilt to make a label.

Lesson One: SINGLE CUT

ODDS AND ENDS, by Jane Boyer.

The skills and techniques taught in this section are the basis for all of the projects. There are three lessons: single cut, multiple cuts, and arcs and half circles. The techniques for the three overlap in many instances, but they have enough distinctions so that separate lessons will be helpful. The stitching and pressing techniques are the same for all three, and these are explained in detail in Lesson One. You will want to do the lessons in the order they are presented. Knowledge gained from the first one is used in the others. Keep all your samples and remnants, as you practice the lessons, to use in the Lesson Project, ODDS AND ENDS SAMPLER, page 22. You will find fabric requirements for the project on page 24.

Cutting Curves from Straight Pieces – Debbie Bowles

Scared to Cut?

Having watched quilters make their first curved cut, I know that some of you will be anxious about doing it "right." Remember, it is only two 6" pieces of fabric, and if you are really having trouble starting, get out some really unlovable fabric and practice!

If you are worried about getting too close to the edges of the strip, lay yardsticks on the long edges to cover the strip by about 1½". The area between the rulers is the cutting space. Your gentle curve will probably measure 10"–15" between the low spot on one curve to the high spot on the next. It has been interesting to note how very similar most of the curves are.

You could also practice by cutting strips of newspaper with an old rotary blade. In my classes, I also suggest using a retracted blade or just your finger to pretend cutting the curve.

Do not draw a curve on the fabric. What happens then is that, rather than cutting a nice, easy flowing curve, you will go slow, the fabric will push forward, and the cut will have jagged places as you try to make the cutter follow the long drawn curve.

Before you begin

Fabric should be pre-washed and measure at least 42" wide. Cut strips selvage to selvage; remove selvages.

Always cut multiples of two fabrics, stacked right side up. Put a new blade in your rotary cutter. If your blade is dull, the fabric will move as you cut, creating distortion/ Use ¼" seam allowances.

Creating the cut

In the single-cut method, one gently curving line is cut up the center of a pair of fabric strips. Curves are randomly placed.

- ○ Cut a 6" x 42" strip from each of two fabrics (A and B).

- ○ Layer A and B strips together *right side up*. The strips must be identical in length. Trim the ends, if needed.

- ○ Starting at the bottom edge, make a cut by randomly "driving" the rotary cutter the length of the strips to create gentle curves.

◆ *Because the width of the strips will be trimmed after piecing, the cut needs to stay about 1½" from the long edges. Gradual curves, not sharp curves, are the goal. When you get to the end of the mat, carefully pull the stack toward you and continue cutting.*

- ○ After cutting, pick up the top piece of one of the sections and place it on the bottom. The cut pieces are now in visible stitching order. A and B on top form a section. A and B on the bottom form another section.

Cutting Curves from Straight Pieces – Debbie Bowles

Sewing the cut

I do not recommend pinning for two reasons. The seam allowance will slip while stitching, and it is easy to stitch a fold into the seam.

○ Always sew together two unlike fabrics. Begin with the two top pieces from the layered fabrics. Place fabric B on top of A, right sides together.

If your cut begins with a curve, you must off-set the top piece ¼" to start the seam. If your cut starts fairly straight, there is no need to offset the pieces. Offsetting allows the curved edges to match.

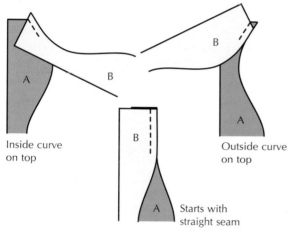

Inside curve on top

Outside curve on top

Starts with straight seam

○ Align the beginning edge of the curve, off-setting the top piece, if needed. Sew the seam until the curved edges no longer align, then stop with the needle down.

○ Lift the presser foot and gently bring the top fabric over to match the curve. Take a few more stitches until the edges no longer align and move the fabric again. Continue sewing this way to join A and B.

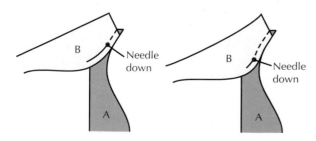

◆ *No pulling! Pulling will make the edges fit, but the distortion will appear in another part of the strip. For the sharpest part of the curve, you will stop and lift the presser foot many times, and you may be taking only three to five stitches at a time. Keep your eye on the curve of the bottom fabric. That is the line you are following.*

○ Use the same method to sew the second pair of sections. You can chain stitch, if you like.

You may find that the sections don't align perfectly at the ends of the stitching line. These variations have been allowed for, and they will be trimmed later.

Pressing the cut

○ Place the pieced strip on the ironing board, right side up, with the dark fabric away from you. Use your fingers to adjust the seam allowance toward darker fabric. Press seam with an up and down motion.

Do not drive your iron around the curves. You will end up with distortion. Do press the seams flat. The curve is easily pressed in either direction. When working on projects with multiple cuts, never press a raw curved edge, which will stretch the fabric.

○ If you find a bulge in the seam after pressing the strips, clip the curves in the seam allowance as shown below.

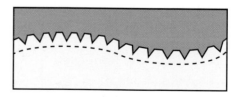

Trimming strips

○ Place a sewn strip on a rotary-cutting mat. Fold it in half crosswise, placing the fold

Cutting Curves from Straight Pieces – Debbie Bowles

on a line on the mat. The piece can be folded with right or wrong sides together. When folded, the raw edges will probably not match perfectly. If the piece is very distorted, re-press, blocking out the worst of the problems.

Each pattern specifies the final width to trim the sewn strips, but you can decide how much to trim from each edge. Sometimes, this will be decided for you because of where the seams lie on the fabric. Before doing any cutting, use your fingers and eyes to ensure that you will not be trimming into the seam line or the seam allowance around the outside of the strip. Before trimming, adjust and smooth the strip by using the lines on the mat.

○ Trim the width of the strip to 4½". While the strip is still in position, trim the ends square, taking off only what is necessary. Each strip will look slightly different. There is no reason for them to be identical except in width.

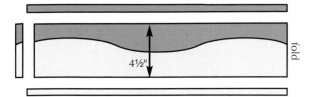

◆ *Although the strip has been straightened, the grain line on the edges is far from true. I handle the pieces gently to avoid distorting the edges. Do not iron the strip after trimming. It is easily stretched.*

Lesson Two: MULTIPLE CUTS

For these blocks, you will need two fat quarters. Several cuts are made the length of the layered pieces. Again, gently curving random cuts will produce the best results.

Cutting strips

○ Trim fat quarters C and D to 16" x 18". For the sampler project, you will not use the trimmings, but you may want to keep them for a future project.

○ Layer C and D, right sides up. Align edges. Make three cuts parallel to the 18" sides, creating four sections. Stay at least 1" from the sides.

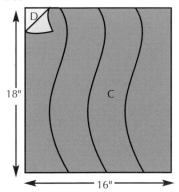

○ To move the sections into sewing order, pick up the top pieces in sections 2 and 4 and move them to the bottom of their respective sections.

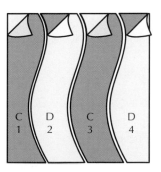

The sections are now in proper sewing order. The four sections on the top will create one block, and the four sections on the bottom will make a second.

Sewing blocks

○ For each block, sew together sections 1 and 2, right sides together, following the lesson for single cuts. Do the same for the first pair of sections in the bottom layer.

○ Press the sewn sections as described on page 11 with the straight edge nearest you. *Never press a raw curved edge*, which will distort the edge, making it difficult to add the next section.

○ Add the third section to each block and press the seam allowances as before.

○ Add the remaining section. Press the blocks very flat. If you have any bulges, clip the curve of the seam allowance.

ODDS AND ENDS, by Janice Johnson. In this variation, the circles were appliquéd.

Trimming blocks

The blocks will have scraggly edges after being sewn. Square them to 12½" as follows:

○ Square the left edge, taking off only what is necessary.

○ Trim the width to 12½". The segment you cut off will be approximately 5"–5½" wide. Save these pieces for the ODDS AND ENDS SAMPLER project.

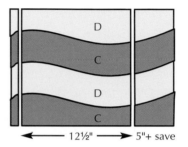

○ Rotate the block and trim the two remaining edges to measure 12½". Each block can be trimmed to your taste, you are not trying to make them identical. Be careful not to cut into the seam or the seam allowance when trimming

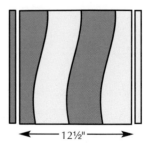

◆ *Do not press the completed blocks after they have been trimmed. The edges are not on the straight of grain, so they could be distorted by pressing.*

Lesson Three:
ARCS and
HALF CIRCLES

Arcs and half circles are created by using the same techniques of marking, cutting, piecing, and pressing that were used in Lessons One and Two. Arc sections start with rectangles. To make half circles, start with squares. For the sampler project on page 22, you will be making half-circle blocks, but arc sections are used in some of the projects.

Making half-circle blocks

○ Cut a 10" strip from each of two fabrics (E and F). Cut two 10" squares each from the E and F strips. Save the remainders.

○ Layer one E and one F square, right side up.

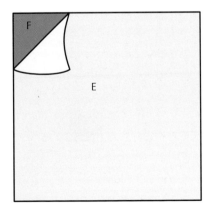

If you are using directional fabrics for half-circle blocks, half of the directional fabric squares must be turned in opposite directions from each other when layered. Then when the two blocks are joined, the fabric pattern will run in the same direction in both halves of the circle.

○ Fold the *left* side of the squares over the right side, aligning the edges carefully. You will be cutting through four layers.

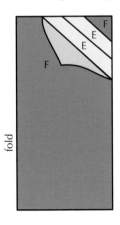

By folding the fabric, you will be assured that the arc is symmetrical because the fold represents the center of the arc. All arc instructions will specify where to mark the beginning and the center of the arc for cutting. Note that the very top of the arc flattens and ends quite straight as it approaches the fold. You can try sketching a half circle on paper to help you visualize this.

○ For the sampler project, mark on the fold 5" down from the top left edge and 2" up from the bottom-right corner. Draw a curve between the two marks, then cut the arc on the drawn line.

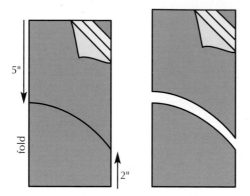

○ Unfold the squares and prepare for sewing by taking half-circle E and placing it under half-circle F. The sections are now in sewing order. The top two fabrics will make one half-circle block, and the bottom two fabrics will make another.

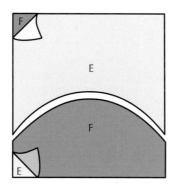

○ With right sides together, sew E to F, using the techniques for stitching curves given on page 16.

◆ *Arc and half circle cuts are tight curves, which require more stopping and repositioning of the fabric during sewing. Also, they usually require clipping the seam allowances to lie flat.*

○ Repeat all steps with the two remaining 10" squares.

○ Press the blocks very flat. A block will usually lie the flattest if the seam allowances are pressed toward the half circle.

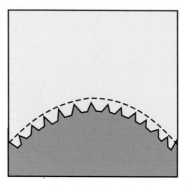

Trimming blocks

Half-circle blocks are trimmed two at a time to create two half circles that appear the same. Center the blocks on a rotary cutting mat to ensure the circle is centered.

Rectangular arc sections are usually trimmed one at a time. The arc sections should be placed on a rotary-cutting mat with the top of the arc centered.

○ *With right sides together,* layer two identical blocks, aligning them with the lines on the cutting mat and with each other. Use your fingers to feel that the seam lines are directly on top of each other.

○ Trim off fairly equal amounts from both the left and right sides to keep the arc centered in the block. Trim to 8½".

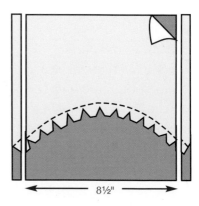

Cutting Curves from Straight Pieces – Debbie Bowles

The top and bottom trimming determine how big the circle looks in the finished block. Some project instructions will tell you where to align your ruler. Some will leave the decision to you. Trim the bottom edge of the half circle first, trimming off only what is necessary to square the edge. Trim the top edge to the measurement specified for the block.

○ For Odds and Ends Sampler, after squaring the bottom edge, trim total width to 8½".

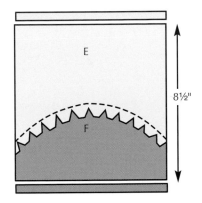

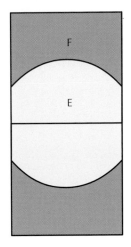 After the blocks have been squared, do not press them. The edges are not on the straight of grain and can be distorted.

The two blocks that were trimmed together are usually sewn together to form one complete circle block. If not stitching now, pin together until you are ready to sew them.

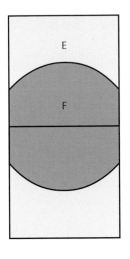

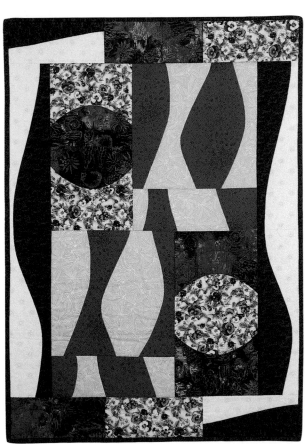

Pansies for Val, by Janice Johnson.

Cutting Curves from Straight Pieces – Debbie Bowles

Lesson Project:
Odds and Ends Sampler

28" x 40"
Two 12" blocks
Four 8" blocks

This handsome sampler is made from the lesson practice pieces and remnants. The lessons start on page 14. Start with a group of six fabrics. Look at the photo and see that the fabrics are used in pairs. Taken separately, each pair contains a fairly high degree of contrast.

The author's quilt was first stitched in the ditch along the block and the border seam lines with monofilament thread. Random curved stitching lines sewn in cotton and specialty threads were added.

ODDS AND ENDS, by the author.

Cutting Curves from Straight Pieces – Debbie Bowles

Fabric Requirements

Cut strips selvage to selvage.

Fabrics	Yards	Cut
A & B	¼ each	one 6" strip each
C & D	fat quarter each	—
E & F	⅜ each	one 10" strip each
Binding	⅜	four 2¼" strips
Backing	1⅜	one 32" x 44" panel
Batting	—	32" x 44"

Making blocks

○ Follow the lessons, beginning on page 14, to make these pieces:
   Two 4½"-wide single-curve A/B strips about 40" long
   Two 12½" x 12½" multiple-curve C/D blocks
   Two C/D remainders, about 5½" x 14½" (may be shorter)
   Four half-circle E/F blocks, 8½" x 8½"
   One E and F remainder, about 10" x 22"

○ Cut both A/B strips to 32½" in length. Save the remainders for the border.

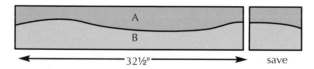

○ Cut both pieced C/D fat-quarter remainders to a width of 4½", then trim the length to 12½". Where the segment is trimmed will affect its appearance.

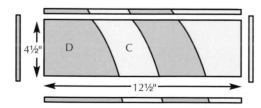

○ From the fabric E remainder, cut one 4½" x 22" strip, From this strip, cut two 7½" segments. From the fabric F remainder, cut two 4½" strips about 22" long.

Quilt assembly

Pin seams to prevent the edges from being distorted. Press seam allowances in any direction unless otherwise noted.

○ Sew the half-circle blocks together to create two rectangular circle blocks.

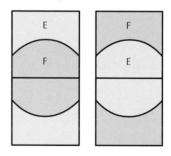

○ Sew the C/D blocks to C/D remainders. Sew the circle blocks to C/D sections.

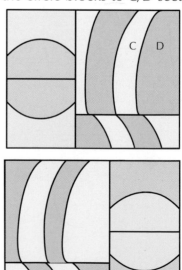

Cutting Curves from Straight Pieces – Debbie Bowles

○ Sew the two sections together. The quilt should measure 20½" x 32½". Square the corners and straighten the edges.

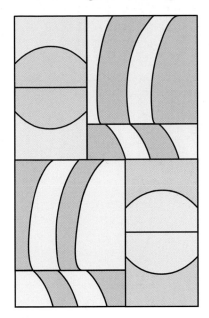

Adding borders

The length of the A/B remainders will vary. Press seam allowances toward the border.

○ Match the centers of the 32½" A/B strips to the centers of the quilt edge, pin often and stitch.

○ Sew a fabric F strip to an A/B remainder. Press seam allowances toward F. From the F strip side, trim to 21½". Make two.

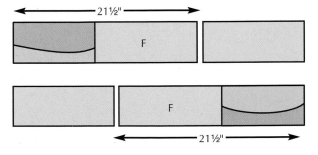

○ Add a 7½" E segment to each strip. Press seam allowances toward E. The pieced border strips should measure 28½".

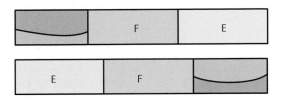

○ Sew the pieced border strips to the top and bottom of the quilt. Press seam allowances the toward border. Square the corners and straighten the edges.

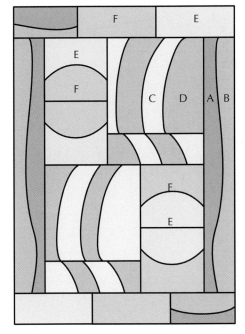

Quilt assembly

Finishing

○ Layer the backing, batting, and quilt top and baste the layers.

○ Quilt the layers and bind the raw edges.

Cutting Curves from Straight Pieces – Debbie Bowles

Pagodas Variations
Wallhanging I

32" x 32"
Four 12" blocks

The pagoda projects are fun to work on because there are so many design options – dark fabric toward the center, light fabric toward the center, some of each, various block placements, and block rotation. Your design wall will really get a workout with any of the Pagodas projects, and you will probably wish you had a second set of blocks. For the best effect, all three fabrics, A, B, and C, should contrast with each other.

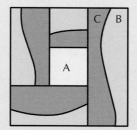 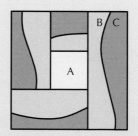

Every pair of 6" fabric strips will make two 12" blocks. It is easy to plan additional sizes of Pagoda quilts. The more blocks you make, the more B/C remainders will be available for the borders. A queen-sized quilt 84" x 108" can be made with 35 blocks and 12" borders. You will need to start with 18 strips cut from each of two different fabrics for the queen size. Many projects use remainders in the border, and the look of the border is easily redesigned by changing the location of the segments.

*PAGODAS Wallhanging I, by the author.
Marbled fabric by Marjorie Behvis.*

Cutting Curves from Straight Pieces – Debbie Bowles

Fabric Requirements

Cut strips selvage to selvage.

Fabrics	Yards	First Cut	Second Cut
A	¼	one 4½" strip	four 4½" squares
B	½	two 6" strips	—
C	½	two 6" strips	—
D	⅜	two 4½" strips	two equal segments each
E	¼	one 4½" strip	four 4½" squares
Binding	⅜	four 2¼" strips	—
Backing	1	36" x 36"	—
Batting	—	36" x 36"	—

All Quilt Sizes

Making blocks

○ Cut and sew single-cut strips from fabrics B and C by following the directions in the lessons. To achieve the most variety, layer and cut only two fabrics at a time. Remember to place fabrics right side up.

○ Trim all B/C strips to 4½" wide.

Before sewing the blocks, decide which fabric will be on the outside. For instance, in the nine-block quilt, page 30, the four corner blocks have the darker fabric on the outside. The remaining blocks have the lighter fabric on the outside. A variety of designs will become possible depending on fabric placement.

○ For each block, from the B/C strips, cut one 4½" segment, two 8½" segments, and one 12½" segment. Save the remainders from the B/C strips for the border.

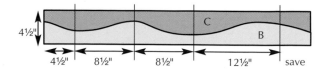

The B/C segments are stitched Log Cabin style, working around the block counter-clockwise. Press the seam allowances away from the center. Keep your iron away from the cut edges as much as possible.

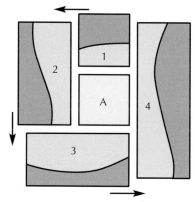

○ Sew a 4½" B/C segment to the top of the center square.

○ Rotate the block counterclockwise and add an 8½" segment. Repeat.

○ Rotate the block again and add the 12½" segment to the last edge. Square the block to 12½" x 12½".

Quilt assembly

○ Make the number of blocks needed for the size quilt you have chosen.

Cutting Curves from Straight Pieces – Debbie Bowles

○ Refer to the quilt photos for assembly. Sew the blocks together in rows, then sew the rows together. Square the corners and straighten the raw edges.

Adding borders

For all borders, arrange the B/C remainders around the quilt, deciding which fabric you like on the outside. Find the center of the border strip and match it to the center of the quilt. The edges are not always on the grain line and may stretch, so place pins fairly close together.

Four-block wallhanging:

○ Square the ends of the B/C remainders, taking off only what is necessary. They may be different lengths.

○ Sew a fabric D segment to one end of each B/C remainder. Press toward D.

○ Trim all pieced border strips to 24½" and sew two to opposite sides of the quilt.

○ Sew a 4½" E square to both ends of each remaining border strip. Press seam allowances toward center. Strips measure 32½".

○ Sew the strips to the top and bottom of the quilt, which should measure 32½" x 32½". Press seam allowances toward border.

Finishing All Quilts

○ If the backing has two panels, cut the yardage in half, selvage to selvage. Trim the selvages from the panels and sew them together along one long side. Press the seam allowances open.

○ Layer the backing, batting, and quilt top and baste.

○ Quilt the layers and bind the raw edges.

The author's quilt (photo, page 27) was first stitched in the ditch on all block seam lines. Additional quilting lines follow the curve of the center block and radiate outward. For a different look, try random gently curved lines quilted diagonally in both directions across the quilt.

You can create randomly pieced binding by cutting 2¼" strips from excess fabric and piecing them end to end to make a strip at least 138" long.

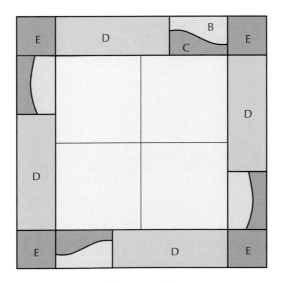

Quilt assembly

Cutting Curves from Straight Pieces – Debbie Bowles

Pagodas Wallhanging II

48" x 48"
Nine 12" blocks

PAGODAS Wallhanging II, by the author.

Cutting Curves from Straight Pieces – Debbie Bowles

Fabric Requirements
Cut strips selvage to selvage.

Fabrics	Yards	First Cut	Second Cut
A	¼	one 4½" strip	nine 4½" squares
B	1	five 6" strips	—
C	1	five 6" strips	—
D	⅜	four 2½" strips	two 36½" segments
		—	two 40½" segments
E	⅝	four 4½" strips	four 30½" segments
Binding	½	five 2¼" strips	—
Backing	3⅛	two 27" x 52" panels	—
Batting	—	52" x 52"	—

Quilt assembly

Follow the instructions (page 28) to make nine blocks. Save one B/C strip for border. Sew blocks together in three rows of three.

Inner border:

○ From the 2½" D strips, cut two 36½" segments and two 40½" segments.

○ Sew the 36½" segments to the sides of the quilt first. Then sew the 40½" segments to the top and bottom. The quilt should measure 40½" x 40½".

Outer border:

○ From unused B/C strip, cut four 9½" segments. Trim four B/C remainders to 5½".

○ From the 4½" E strips, cut four 30½" long segments.

○ Sew 5½" B/C remainders to the ends of two 30½" E segments and sew these borders to the sides of the quilt. Sew the 9½" B/C remainders to the ends of the remaining E segments. Sew these to the top and bottom. The quilt measures 48½" x 48½".

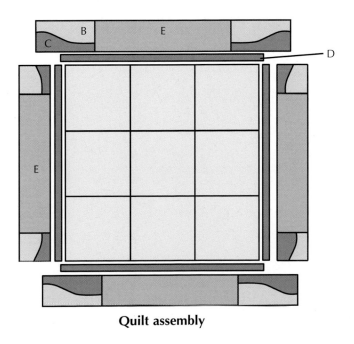

Quilt assembly

Cutting Curves from Straight Pieces – Debbie Bowles

Pagodas Lap Quilt

60" x 72"

Twenty 12" blocks

PAGODAS Lap Quilt, by Sandra Tundel.

Cutting Curves from Straight Pieces – Debbie Bowles

Fabric Requirements
Cut strips selvage to selvage.

Fabrics	Yards	First Cut	Second Cut
A	½	three 4½" strips	twenty 4½" squares
B & C	2	ten 6" strips each	—
D	⅝	six 2½" strips	—
E	⅝	four 4½" strips	—
Binding	⅝	seven 2¼" strips	—
Backing	3¾	two 39" x 64" panels	—
Batting	—	64" x 76"	—

Quilt assembly

Make 20 blocks and sew them together in a four by five setting (instructions start on page 28).

Inner border:

○ Sew together three 2½" strips of fabric D, end to end. Press seam allowances open.

○ Cut two 60½" segments from this strip and sew them to the sides of the quilt.

○ Sew the other three 2½" strips of fabric D together. Cut two 52½" segments and sew them to the top and bottom. The quilt now measures 52½" x 64½".

Outer border:

○ Square the ends of the B/C remainders, taking off only what is necessary. Segments will vary in length. Sew segments together in groups of two or three as shown in the quilt assembly diagram.

○ Position the groups around the quilt edge and measure the space between them. Cut the fabric E strips 2" longer than you need to allow for the seam allowances and error. Stitch four borders. Press seam allowances toward E. Trim the side borders to 64½" and sew them to the quilt. Press seam allowances toward borders.

○ Trim the top and bottom borders to 60½". Sew them to the quilt. The quilt measures 60½" x 72½".

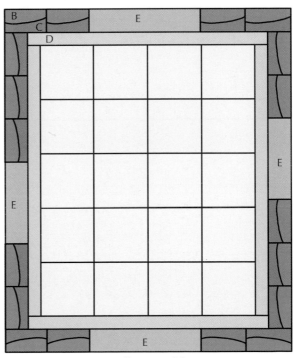

Quilt assembly

Unique Pagodas

60" x 72"
Twenty 12" blocks

This variation of the PAGODAS quilt is created by using 20 fabrics for the 20 blocks. Each fabric appears in three blocks: as a center square, an inside edge, and an outside edge. The directions highlight only the steps that are different from the original PAGODAS on page 27. All the sizes in the original could be adapted to this style.

UNIQUE PAGODAS, by the author.

Cutting Curves from Straight Pieces – Debbie Bowles

Fabric Requirements

Cut strips selvage to selvage.
Blocks: Choose 20 fabrics in an assortment of lights, mediums,
and darks: ¼ yard each; cut one 6" strip from each.

Fabrics	Yards	Cut
Border (A & B)	1⅞ each	two 9" strips each, parallel to selvages (65")
Binding	—	two 2¼" light strips, parallel to selvages
		three 2¼" dark strips, parallel to selvages
Backing	3¾	two 39" x 64" panels
Batting	—	64" x 76"

Making blocks

○ From each of the twenty 6" strips, cut one 4½" square.

○ Sort the squares and strips into pairs and choose two squares for each group. Check for good contrast.

○ Use the single-cut method, described in the lessons, to cut gentle curves in each pair of strips. Cut only one pair of strips at a time to create as many different curves as possible.

○ Piece the blocks as directed in PAGODAS, pages 28 and 29, to create twenty unique blocks.

Quilt assembly

○ Sew blocks together in rows of four. Make five rows.

○ Sew the rows together. Square the corners and straighten the raw edges. The quilt measures 48½" x 60½".

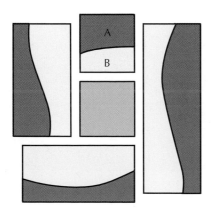

Cutting Curves from Straight Pieces – Debbie Bowles

Adding borders

Tip: *To cut long border strips parallel to the selvage, double fold the fabrics along their length, or use a pencil and ruler, to mark two guide lines for cutting.*

○ For the border, layer one A and one B strip right sides up. Using the lesson directions for multiple curves, make two cuts, to create three sections.

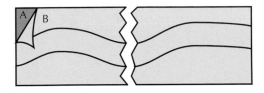

○ Sew different colored sections together and press. Repeat for the remaining A/B strips. Trim the A/B strips to 6½" x 60½". Strips will need to be double-folded to trim the width.

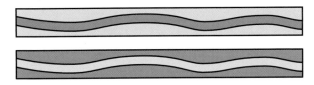

Neither the quilt edge nor the borders are on the straight of grain. Remember to handle carefully.

○ The side borders are added first. Match the centers of the border strips with the centers of the quilt edges. Pin generously and sew both borders to the quilt, pressing seam allowances toward the borders. The quilt measures 60½" x 60½".

○ Pin, sew, and press the top and bottom borders as you did for the side borders. The quilt measures 60½" x 72½".

Finishing

○ Layer, baste, and quilt as described for PAGODAS, on page 29.

○ For UNIQUE PAGODAS, wavy diagonal quilting lines run in both directions from border to border.

○ To create the binding pictured, lay strips around the quilt, joining A/B binding strips at the locations of your choice. You will need approximately 142" of dark binding, slightly less of light.

Quilt assembly

Double Pagodas

**Lap Quilt
56" x 84"
Fifteen 16" blocks**

Choosing colors and arranging the blocks make this a fun project. The quilt combines curved lines with a traditional straight-line favorite, the Log Cabin block, and you will find that a wonderful variety of block settings are possible. The lap quilt on the facing page has high contrast in the two color families and in the lights and darks within the families, creating a bold look.

The quilt instructions for the lap quilt call for making 16 blocks. Consider using the extra block as an interesting quilt label or a pillow, or use all 16 blocks in a project set four by four or two by eight. The four-block size would make a fun oversized pillow top or wallhanging. Try using a stripe for one of the fabrics.

For a larger project, consider using multiple fabrics for each color family, for instance, a group of dark blues rather than just one. You could also make larger blocks by adding another row around the perimeter. There are a lot of possibilities.

DOUBLE PAGODAS Lap Quilt, by the author; quilted by Brenda Leino.

Cutting Curves from Straight Pieces – Debbie Bowles

Fabric Requirements

Cut strips selvage to selvage.

Fabrics	Yards	Cut
A	⅜	two 4½" strips
B (dark)	1⅞	nine 4½" strips
outer border		seven 2½" strips
C (light)	1⅝	nine 4½" strips
inner border		four 2½" strips
D (light)	1½	ten 4½" strips
E (dark)	1½	ten 4½" strips
Binding	¾	eight 2¼" strips
Backing	5¼	two 31" x 89" panels
Batting	—	61" x 89"

Making blocks

The strips are narrow so the curves need to be shallow and gentle. There is only about ½" to trim from the width after piecing.

○ Cut sixteen 4½" squares from the A strips for the block centers.

○ Using the 4½" strips, layer one B and one C strip right sides up. Cut a single curve, as described in the lessons, staying at least 1" from the long edges.

○ Place the strips in sewing order and sew the curved sections together. Press the seams.

○ Trim the strips to 3½" wide. Square the ends, taking off only what is necessary. Make eighteen B/C strips. Repeat the instructions to make twenty D/E strips.

Tip: If your pieced strips are 42" or longer after trimming, you will have extra strips.

○ From sixteen B/C strips, cut two 10½" segments and one 16½" segment, then cut sixteen 4½" segments from the two remaining strips.

○ From the D/E strips, cut these segments: thirty-two 7½" and thirty-two 13½".

The blocks are pieced Log Cabin style, working counterclockwise around the center square. The B/C segments are sewn with the darker fabric (B) toward the center. The D/E segments are sewn with the lighter fabric (D) toward the center. Press all seam allowances away from the center. You can chain stitch the segments, pressing each one before adding the next. The edges are not on the straight of grain and should be pinned to prevent stretching.

○ Arrange the segments and center squares in blocks. Chain-sew to make sixteen blocks. Square them to 16½".

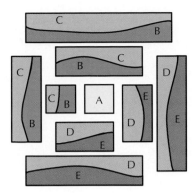

Quilt assembly

The blocks are arranged three across by five down. Alternate the direction the seam allowances are pressed for crisp intersections at the block seams.

Entire books are devoted to the different settings possible with Log Cabin blocks. Any setting can be duplicated with Double Pagoda blocks, and it is great fun to try various ones before deciding on a particular setting.

- Sew the blocks in five rows of three blocks each, then sew the rows together. The top should measure 48½" x 80½". Square the corners and straighten the edges.

- For the borders, sew two B strips together, end to end. Press seam allowances open and trim the sewn strip to 80½". Make two of these. Repeat for the C border strips.

- Sew a B and a C strip together on one long edge. Press the seam allowances toward B. Repeat for the other pair of strips.

- Sew the C edge of the border strips to the long sides of the quilt top, pinning frequently. Press seam allowances toward the borders.

- Sew three B strips together, end to end. Cut the resulting strip into two 56½" lengths.

- Sew the 56½" B strips to the top and bottom of the quilt and press seam allowances toward the border. The quilt now measures 56½" x 84½".

Finishing

- Cut the backing yardage in half, selvage to selvage, creating two lengths of fabric. Sew them together on one long edge. Press the seam allowances open.

- Layer the backing, batting, and quilt top and baste. Quilt the layers and bind the raw edges.

To the quilter, Brenda, the red strips looked like flames when she first looked at this quilt top, so that is how she proceeded with her quilting design. She used cotton and rayon threads.

Quilt assembly

DOUBLE PAGODAS Wallhanging
38" x 38", Four 16" blocks
For expanded directions, see page 40, Double Pagodas.

Fabric Requirements
Cut strips selvage to selvage.

Fabrics	Yards	Cut
A	¼	one 4½" strip
B	½	three 4½" strips
C	½	three 4½" strips
D	½	three 4½" strips
E	½	three 4½" strips
Border	½	four 3½" strips
Binding	⅜	four 2¼" strips
Backing	1¼	42" x 42"
Batting	—	42" x 42"

Making blocks

○ Cut four 4½" squares from the A strip for the centers of the blocks. Use the single-cut method described in the lessons to cut gentle curves in each pair of strips.

○ Sew curved sections together to make six B/C strips and six D/E strips.

○ From the B/C strips, cut four 4½", eight 10½", and four 16½" segments.

○ From the D/E strips, cut eight 7½" and eight 13½" segments.

○ Sew the squares and segments together to make four blocks. Square to 16½".

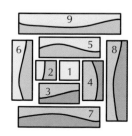

Quilt assembly

○ Sew the blocks together, two across by two down. Alternate the direction the seam allowances are pressed for crisp seam intersections. Square the corners and straighten the edges. The quilt top measures 32½" x 32½".

Quilt assembly

○ From the four border strips, cut two 32½" and two 38½" lengths.

○ Pinning frequently, sew the 32½" segments to the quilt sides. Sew the 38½" segments to top and bottom. Press seam allowances toward the borders.

○ Square the corners and straighten the edges. The quilt measures 38½" x 38½".

Finishing

○ Layer the backing, batting, and quilt top and baste the layers. Quilt the layers and bind the raw edges.

Double Pagodas Wallhanging, by the author.

Cutting Curves from Straight Pieces – Debbie Bowles

Strings and Squares

12" x 38"
Table Runner

Small table runners like these stitch up very quickly and give you a chance to dress your table for a holiday or just an any-day tea party. To make the runner longer, buy the length of fabric you need plus 2" and cut the strips parallel to the selvage.

STRINGS AND SQUARES Table Runner, by Sandra Tundel.

Cutting Curves from Straight Pieces – Debbie Bowles

Fabric Requirements

Cut strips selvage to selvage.

Fabrics	Yards	Cut
A	⅜	one 6" strip one 4" strip
B	⅜	one 6" strip one 4" strip
Accents	—	ten to fifteen 2" squares
Binding (optional)	¼	three 2¼" strips
Backing	½	16" x 42"

Cutting curves

○ Layer the 6" A and B strips right sides up.

○ Using the single-cut method, as described in the lessons, cut a gently curving line along the length of the strips.

○ Place the curved sections in sewing order. Sew each pair together.

○ Trim the width to 4½" and the length to 38½". Repeat cutting directions with the 4" strips of A and B.

○ Trim the width of the strips to 2½" and the length to 38½".

Quilt assembly

○ Referring to the illustration for placement, sew the four strips together, pinning generously. The piece measures 12½" x 38½".

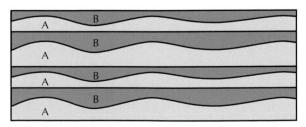

Turned edges

Use the following instructions for a turned finish, as you would use for making a pillow. (The edges can be bound, if you prefer.)

○ With right sides together, center the table runner on the backing. Pin generously. Sew ¼" from the edges of the table runner, leaving an unstitched opening for turning the piece right side out.

○ Trim the excess backing even with the edges of the table runner and turn the piece right side out. Press the edges flat. Hand stitch the opening closed.

○ Optional: top stitch around the table runner, ¼" from edge.

Finishing

○ Position the accent squares and sew them in place with a small zigzag, decorative stitch, or fusing. Add additional stitching or appliqué if you desire.

○ If you have chosen to bind the edges, cut three 2¼" strips. Sew strips together end to end to make at least 110" of continuous binding.

Cutting Curves from Straight Pieces – Debbie Bowles

Satisfaction

Wallhanging
37½" x 46½"

Sometimes less really is more. SATISFACTION has simple, clean lines, but what a bold and dramatic look you can achieve. This is the first project I created with inventive curved cutting. I find that many quilters have a special fabric in their collections that they are just waiting to showcase like this.

The size of your project depends only on your imagination. Using just the width of the fabric, the strips could be up to 42" long. For longer strips, just cut from the length of the fabric, parallel to the selvages. You can then make the strips any length you desire. Cut the binding strips at the same time, also from the length of the fabric. Make the quilt longer by adding more strips. Every two strips of fabric will make two pieced strips in reversed colors.

Consider adding a third color to the sashing squares or adding accent squares to the borders as you see in the photo. The border instructions are for solid borders. You can easily insert 3½" squares wherever you want, then trim to the lengths given.

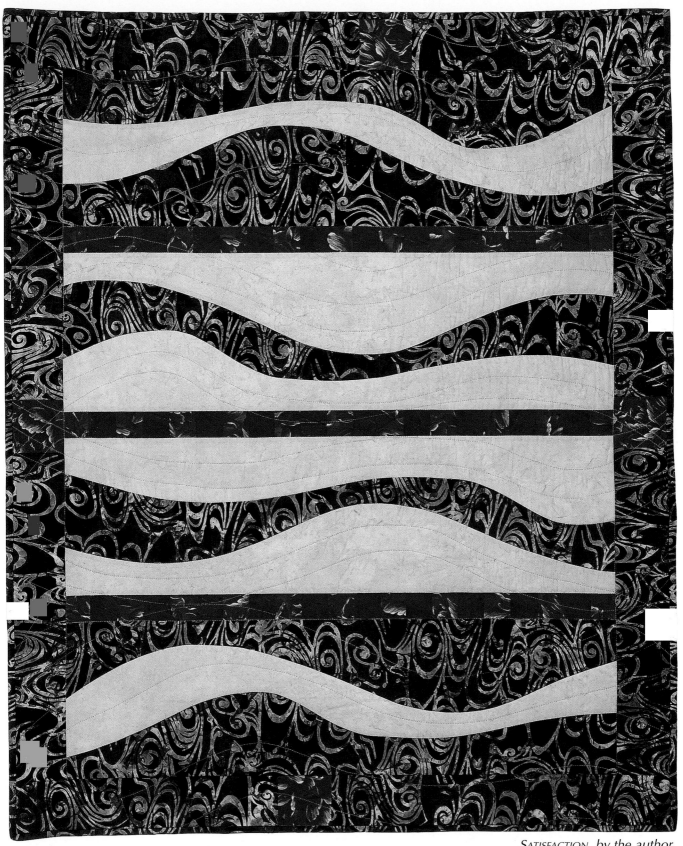

SATISFACTION, by the author.
This piece can also be hung sideways.

Cutting Curves from Straight Pieces – Debbie Bowles

Fabric Requirements

Cut strips selvage to selvage.

Fabrics	Yards	Cut
A	¼	two 2" strips
B	¼	two 2" strips
C	⅞	two 12" strips
D	⅞	two 12" strips
Border	½	four 3½" strips
Binding	⅜	five 2¼" strips
Backing	1½	42" x 51"
Batting	—	42" x 51"

Cutting curves

○ Trim the selvages from the strips. Stack four strips together in this order: C, D, C, and D, all right side up.

○ Check the photo and notice how the area between the cuts narrows and widens. Following the lesson directions for multiple cuts, make two cuts the length of the strips, creating three sections. Stay at least 1½" from the long edges.

○ Put the top piece of the middle section two on the bottom of its stack so the pieces are in sewing order.

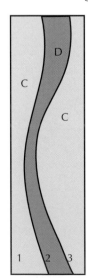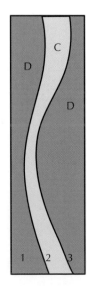

○ When sewing the sections together, press seam allowances toward the unstitched curved edge as each section is added. Complete the four strips.

○ Trim the sewn strips to 9½" x 32". The curve is identical on all the strips. If you want them to look different, cut the 32" from different parts of the strips.

Sashing

○ Sew the four A and B strips together on the long edge, alternating fabrics. Press all the seam allowances in the same direction.

○ Cut strip A/B/A/B in half and sew the halves together side by side. Cut nine 2" segments from the sewn strips.

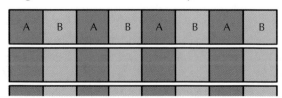

○ Sew three 2" segments together, end to end. Make three of these strips.

○ The strips contain 24 squares each, but only 21 are needed for sashing. Remove three of the squares from each strip.

Cutting Curves from Straight Pieces – Debbie Bowles

Quilt assembly

○ Measure the length of the sashing strips. They should be 32". If they are not, check the seams and make adjustments. The following directions assume 32"-long sashing.

○ Using the quilt assembly diagram as a guide, sew together the curved strips and sashing strips, pinning often and pressing all seam allowances in the same direction. For a different look, rotate some of the curved strips.

○ Square the corners and straighten the edges. The piece measures 32" x 41".

Adding borders

○ From border strips, cut two 41" segments for the side borders and sew to the quilt. Square the corners.

○ Cut two borders 38" each and stitch to quilt. Square the corners. The quilt measures 38" x 47".

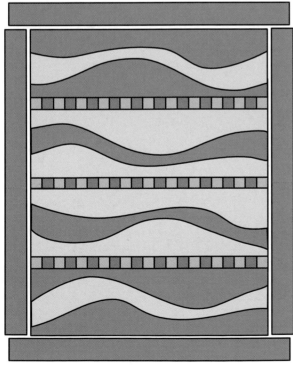

Quilt assembly

Finishing

○ Layer the backing, batting, and quilt top and baste the layers.

○ Quilt the layers and bind the raw edges.

The pictured quilt on page 47 was first stitched in the ditch along all the seam lines. Additional quilting lines follow the curves of each strip and extend into the border.

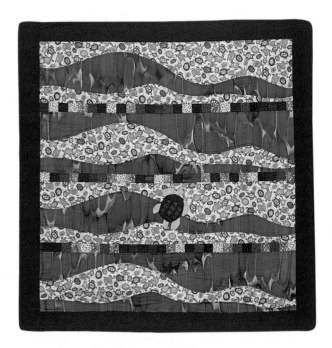

SATISFACTION and detail, by Pat Eastlund. Pat added an appliqué turtle to her quilt.

Parade

Tablecloth
48" x 68"

The Fourth of July is a big holiday for us. Most of my family comes for the holiday, which includes my son Ryan's birthday and a parade with the neighborhood marching band. A festive tablecloth is just what is needed for these summer holiday meals.

This tablecloth is simple and easy to make, with just a little care as to fabric placement. (See "Sewing Tips" on page 55 for making waves and stars.) When my critique group tried out this design, we each made a row, which was a fun group project.

PARADE, by the author.

Cutting Curves from Straight Pieces – Debbie Bowles

Fabric Requirements

Cut strips selvage to selvage. See Sewing Tips, page 55.

Fabrics	Yards	Cut
A	1½	seven 6" strips
B	1¾	seven 6" strips
border 1		five 2½" strips
C (stars)	¾	three 4½" strips
D Border 2	1	six 4½" strips
Backing	3	two 37" x 52" panels

Cutting curves

◐ Make 14 single-curve A/B strips. Trim the strips to 4½" wide.

◐ From the C strips, cut 25 4½" squares. Mark 20 of them with a diagonal line, corner to corner, on the wrong side. These will become the star points. The other five squares are the star bodies.

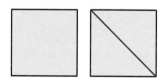

Each A/B strip becomes a row in this quilt. The rows measure 36½". Only the top and bottom rows are used uncut. All other A/B strips are cut into segments to accommodate the star points.

Quilt assembly

◐ Referring to the quilt assembly diagram, make the quilt by rows, as follows:

Row 1: With fabric B at the top of the A/B strip, trim the strip to 36½". Set aside.

Row 2: Place the second strip so that fabric A is at the top. Starting from the left end, cut a 30½" segment and a 6½" segment.

Place a 4½" square on the right end of the 30½" segment as shown below. Sew on the diagonal line. Trim off the bottom two triangles, leaving a ¼" seam allowance. Flip the triangle up and press.

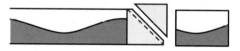

Sew the 30½" and 6½" segments together, then sew row 2 to row 1.

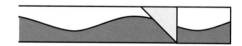

Row 3: With fabric B at the top, cut a 26½" and a 6½" segment. Stitch-and-flip a 4½" square to the right end of the 26½" segment and the left end of the 6½" segment. Sew a 4½" square between the two pieced segments. Join this row to the previous ones.

Row 4: With fabric A at the top, cut a 10½" segment, a 16½" segment, and a 10½" segment. Stitch-and-flip a 4½" square to the right end of the first 10½" segment and the left end of the second 10½" segment. Join the three segments. Join this row to the previous rows.

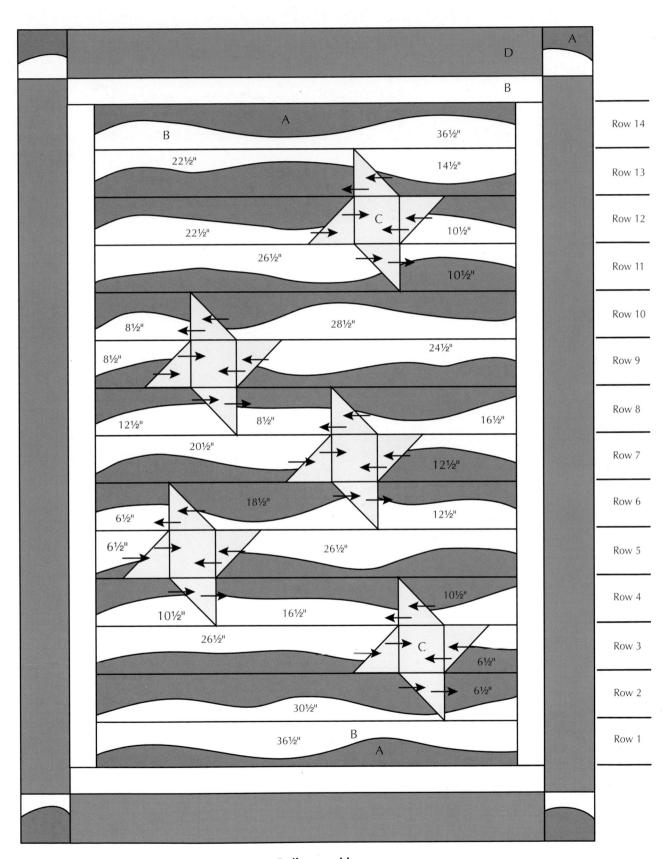

Quilt assembly

Cutting Curves from Straight Pieces – Debbie Bowles

○ You have created one complete star section. Build the remaining rows the same way.

○ Square the corners and straighten the edges. The quilt measures 36½" x 56½".

Adding borders

○ For border 1, join three 2½" strips. Cut two 56½" lengths from the sewn strip.

○ Sew strips to the sides of the quilt and press seam allowances toward the border.

○ Cut two 40½" lengths from the 2½" strips, sew to the top and bottom. Press. Square the corners. Quilt measures 40½" x 60½".

○ Border 2, cut four 4½" squares from the remainders of the pieced A/B strips. Sew

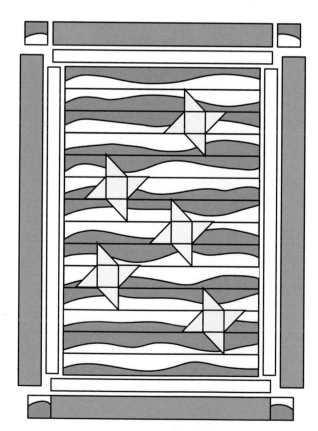

Border assembly

4½" strips together end to end, to make two 60½" lengths.

○ Sew to the sides of the quilt and press the seam allowances toward the border.

○ Cut two 40½" lengths from the 4½" border strips. Sew the 4½" A/B squares to the ends of both segments. Press seam allowances toward border.

○ Sew these strips to the top and bottom of the quilt. Press seam allowances toward the border. Square the corners. The quilt measures 48½" x 68½".

Finishing

○ For a turned finish, cut the backing yardage in half, creating two panels. Trim off the selvages and sew the panels together on one long edge.

○ With right sides together, center the quilt top on the backing. Leave the excess fabric until the quilt edges have been sewn. Pin generously around the perimeter of the quilt top. (There is no batting.)

○ With a ½" seam allowance, sew around the quilt, leaving an opening of about 8" to turn quilt right side out. Backstitch a few stitches at both ends of the opening.

○ Trim the backing even with the raw edges of the quilt top. Turn the quilt and press. Hand stitch the opening closed. Topstitch ¼" around the quilt edge.

○ You will need to do something to the quilt to hold the two layers together. You could tie it, bar tack it, or add decorative stitching by machine or hand. Be sure to pin or baste the quilt before adding any stitching.

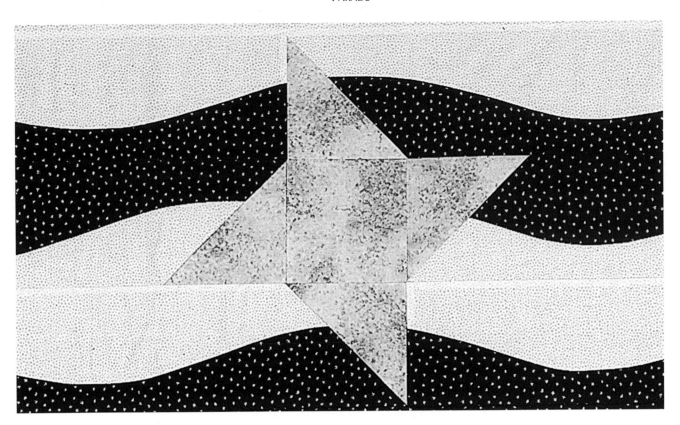

Sewing Tips

Waves

• It's best to avoid directional fabric.

• Cut all the red and white (A/B) segments sequentially, from left to right, to make the waves continuous.

• Place the cut segments on a flat surface, making sure the reds and whites are in the correct positions.

• Piece segments and star parts one row at a time, pressing the seam allowances in the direction of the arrows on the assembly diagram.

• Join rows together as you go, pinning often. Press seam allowances in any direction.

• Check off the rows on the quilt assembly diagram as you complete them.

Stars

• When the star points are sewn to the star body, press seam allowances toward the body.

• To achieve crisp star points, on the wrong side of each row, use a ruler to draw the ¼" seam allowance across the diagonal seams.

• Place a dot at the seam intersections to help you match the seams when pinning the rows together.

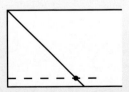

• When joining rows, sew just outside the intersection (one thread width), in the seam allowance.

Cutting Curves from Straight Pieces – Debbie Bowles

Letting Loose

77" x 98"
One hundred twenty-six 6" blocks
Fourteen 6" x 9" rectangles

LETTING LOOSE contains 30 different fabrics. Don't make yourself crazy choosing them because they don't really have to match. This is a wonderful project for trying out unusual color schemes and pushing yourself out of your personal comfort zone, really letting loose!

If you have never tried to pull together this many fabrics, here are some tricks to make it easier. Start with a multicolored print that has the color, look, and feel you like. You can plan to use this print in the quilt or the border, or just use it as a color reference. Study the print and look at the over-all color, the color families, and the accent colors. Choose fabrics that represent these categories, both lighter and darker, changing both the shading and intensity as you select the fabrics. Pick an assortment of large- and small-scale prints, tone-on-tone prints, and anything else that suits you.

With so many fabrics in the blocks, it is difficult to predict what fabric to use for the border. It is usually best to select the border fabric after the quilt top has been pieced. You may find that the quilt has taken on a life of its own during the piecing, and the color family you planned to dominate has taken a back seat to something else.

Every block in your quilt will be different, and the real fun will be during the final design time.

LETTING LOOSE, by the author; quilted by Brenda Leino. The quilt was randomly quilted with large squiggly lines.

Cutting Curves from Straight Pieces – Debbie Bowles

Fabric Requirements

Cut strips selvage to selvage.
Blocks: Choose 30 fabrics – 10 each of lights, mediums, and darks.
You will need ⅜ yard of each. Cut one 10" strip from each fabric.

Fabrics	Yards	Cut
Border 1	¾	eight 2½" strips
Border 2	½	eight 1½" strips
Border 3	1⅜	nine 4½" strips
Binding	¾	nine 2¼" strips
Backing	6	two 41" x 102" panels
Batting	—	81" x 102"

Cutting strips

◔ Organize the strips into groups of three, making sure that each group has a light, a medium, and a dark fabric. The most important element in each group is contrast. The colors in each group do not have to match.

◆ *The following directions are for one group of three fabrics. Begin by working with just one group and complete all the steps for that group. After doing the first strip set, you will have a better idea of the most efficient way for you to work.*

◔ With the right sides up, layer three 10" strips. Using the lesson for multiple cuts on page 17, make two cuts, creating three sections.

If the center curved section is between 3" and 4" wide, you will have a good amount of each fabric showing in the blocks. You will be making nine more sets of pieced strips, so if this first one isn't quite what you like, you will have many more opportunities.

◔ Place the cut strips in sewing order. Each pieced strip will have three different fabrics in three different positions.

◔ Sew and press the strips, following the lesson directions. Do not trim the width at this time.

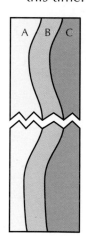  

Sewing blocks

◔ From each pieced strip, cut four 8" segments. Save the remainders of the strips to be used later. Keep the four segments together. Make three sets of four.

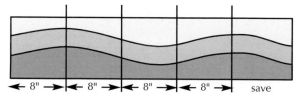

◔ Trim each segment as shown in following figure, creating 8" squares. You are not trying to make the squares look identical to each other, but you do want the center fabric to be close to the center of the block. Make three sets of four 8" squares.

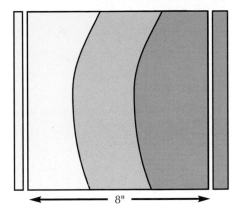

With right sides up, the colors in the same position on each block, and the center stripe running vertically, stack the four squares in a set. Align the edges carefully.

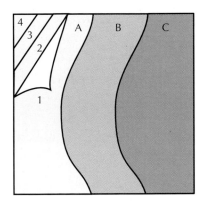

Make two diagonal cuts, corner to corner.

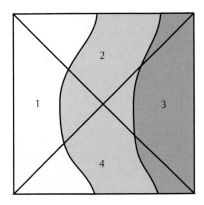

Trying different placements, arrange the triangles to make four blocks. See pages 10–12 for piecing quarter-square trian-

gles. Piece the four blocks. Repeat the steps for the remaining sets of 8" squares. Trim all the blocks to 6½" x 6½".

PLACEMENT POSSIBILITIES

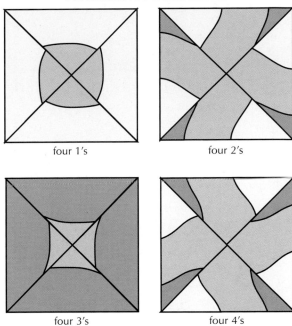

four 1's   four 2's

four 3's   four 4's

The 6½" blocks in the photo were cut from the centers of the 8" squares. If you cut the blocks off-center, you will have a different look.

Follow the previous directions for the nine remaining groups of fabrics.

I prefer to complete each step for all the fabrics before moving on to the next step. You may find it better for you to work with one strip set at a time. If you vary the width and the swoop of the curve, you will create a different look for your blocks. After you finish all ten groups, there will be 120 6½" blocks and thirty curved remainders approximately 8"–12" long.

Curved remainders

From the thirty remainders, find fourteen that are at least 9½" long. Trim them to 9½". A scrap can be pieced to a remainder if it isn't quite long enough.

Cutting Curves from Straight Pieces – Debbie Bowles

○ Trim the width of the curved remainders to 6½". Set the rectangles aside with the blocks.

○ Choose six more remainders and trim them to 6½" x 6½" blocks.

Quilt assembly

○ Refer to the quilt assembly diagram to arrange the blocks and rectangles.

The two types of blocks in the quilt in the photograph are alternated, and contrasting fabrics are spread throughout the quilt. The six blocks created from strip remainders are placed randomly in the quilt. Although I started out to have a pattern for the arrangement of the blocks, as I moved blocks around for color reasons, the pattern became less distinct. What that means is … let loose with your arrangement!

○ Sew all the blocks and rectangles in horizontal rows.

○ Press the seam allowances one row at a time. These seams are not aligned with anything, so they can be pressed in any direction. After pressing each row, place it back on the design area you are using.

For the remainder blocks and rectangles, the seams will lie flatter if they are pressed toward the remainder and away from the "X" blocks.

○ Because the rows have so many seams, it is possible they will not be a uniform length. The rows should measure 63½". Measure each row and make adjustments in the seam allowances, if needed.

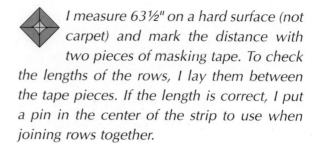 *I measure 63½" on a hard surface (not carpet) and mark the distance with two pieces of masking tape. To check the lengths of the rows, I lay them between the tape pieces. If the length is correct, I put a pin in the center of the strip to use when joining rows together.*

○ Sew the rows of strips together, matching centers and pinning generously to avoid distortion. Remember to square the corners and straighten the edges. The quilt top should measure 63½" x 84½".

The seams between the rows are bulky. I press them open from the back first and then press them firmly from the right side.

Adding borders

○ Measure the quilt for each border addition. Sew border strips together, end to end, and cut the lengths needed from the the sewn strips.

Cut the following border lengths:
Border 1 top and bottom 63½", sides 88½".
Border 2 top and bottom 67½", sides 90½".
Border 3 top and bottom 69½", sides 98½".

○ For each round of borders, sew the top and bottom border strips to the quilt first and then the sides. Press the seam allowances toward the borders. After all the borders have been added, the quilt should measure 77½" x 98½".

Finishing

○ Layer the backing, batting, and quilt top and baste the layers.

○ Quilt the layers and bind the raw edges.

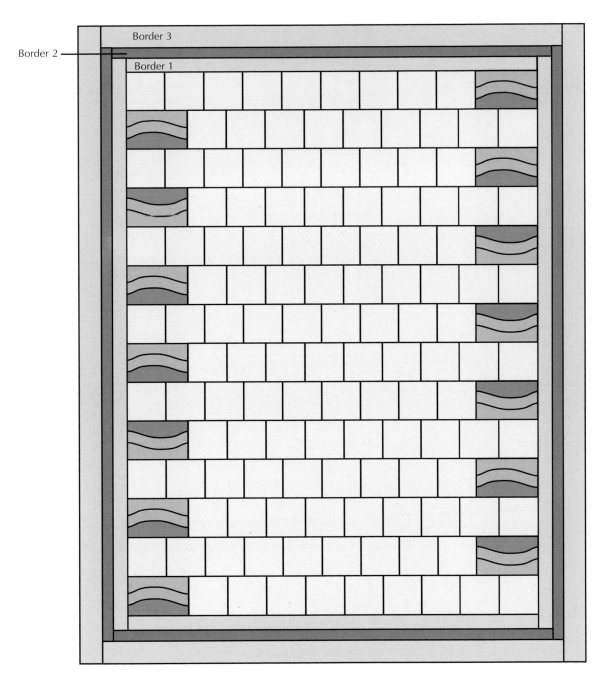

Quilt assembly

Cutting Curves from Straight Pieces – Debbie Bowles

Bent Pieces

18" x 54"
Four 12" blocks
Table Runner

For those quilters who collect fat quarters, here is a project just for you. You can use high or low contrast, and you don't even need to have a color plan. If you are frugal, you'll enjoy using nearly every bit of fabric to create the strips, pieced borders, and binding.

If you want to create a bed-sized quilt, you can easily determine the yardage because every two fat quarters make two blocks, a border, and binding. Start with 48 fat quarters to make a project that is six blocks (72") by eight blocks (96"). Adding the same type of borders as shown in the lap quilt, this quilt would be 83½" x 107½". Consider using a double inner border or a double outer border on two sides to increase the width or length.

BENT PIECES, by the author.

Cutting Curves from Straight Pieces – Debbie Bowles

Fabric Requirements
Cut strips selvage to selvage.

Fabrics	Yards
A	two fat quarters
B	one fat quarter
C	one fat quarter
Border 1	one fat quarter
Border 2	remainders
Binding	⅜ yd., four 2¼" strips
Backing	1 yd., two 21" x 27" panels
Batting	21" x 58"

BENT PIECES
Table Runner
18" x 54"
Four 12" blocks

Making blocks

○ Trim the block fat quarters to 16" x 18" by cutting off a piece approximately 6" x 18". Save the trimmings.

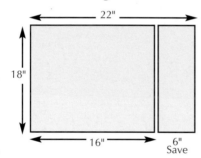

○ Layer one A and B, right side up; align edges.

○ Refer to Lesson Two (page 17) for multiple cuts. Make three cuts parallel to the 18" side, staying at least 1" from the sides.

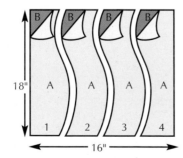

○ Place the sections in sewing order. Stitch and press the sections.

FABRIC TIP
Fat quarters vary slightly in size both before and after pre-washing. Measure your fat quarters after washing. Sometimes, they shrink slightly, and by the time you have squared them, you don't have 18" x 22" of usable fabric. Because these projects use nearly every bit, the fat quarter you start with must be at least 18" x 21".

○ Repeat instructions for fabrics A and C to make two A/B blocks and two A/C blocks.

○ Trim the blocks, in the order shown, to 12½" x 12½", saving the remainders for the border. You are not trying to make them look identical. Do not press the completed blocks after trimming.

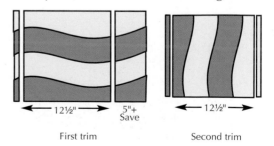

First trim   Second trim

Quilt assembly

◯ The four blocks can be arranged in various ways. Sew blocks together when you have an arrangement you like. Press all seam allowances in the same direction.

◯ Square the corners and straighten the edges. The quilt measures 12½" x 48½".

Adding borders

Border 1:

◯ From fat quarter, cut eight 1½" x 18" strips. From strips, cut two 12½" segments.

◯ Sew the 12½" segments to the top and bottom of the quilt and press the allowances toward the border.

◯ Sew three 18" segments together for each of the side borders. Press allowances open and trim the strips to 50½".

◯ Sew the strips to the sides of the quilt and press the allowances toward the border.

◯ Square the corners and straighten the edges. The quilt measures 14½" x 50½".

Border 2:

◯ Square the short ends of the pieced remainders, taking off as little as possible.

◯ Find one section that is at least 14½" long. If you have none, piece a 2" scrap to one end and trim to 14½". From this section, cut two 2½" x 14½" segments for the top and bottom borders.

◯ Cut the three other remainders into 2½"-wide strips. An exact length is not necessary. Cut six.

◯ Cut 2½" strips from the remainders of fabrics A, B, and C to use as fillers for the side borders to achieve the required length.

◯ Arrange the segments around the quilt. Sew the side border pieces and fillers together, end to end, and trim the strips to 54½" in length.

◯ Sew the top and bottom borders to the quilt and press the allowances toward the borders.

◯ Sew the side borders to the quilt and press allowances outward. The quilt measures 18½" x 54½".

Finishing

◯ Follow the finishing instructions for the lap quilt (page 67), except the backing panels are sewn together on the short ends.

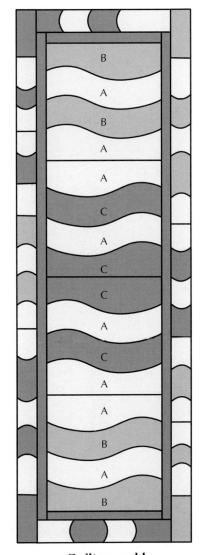

Quilt assembly

Cutting Curves from Straight Pieces – Debbie Bowles

BENT PIECES
Lap Quilt
47½" x 71½"
Fifteen 12" blocks

Fabric Requirements

Cut strips selvage to selvage. Choose 16 fat quarters. Every two fat quarters make two blocks, border, and binding.

Fabrics	Yards	Cut
Backing	3¼	two 38" x 52" panels
Batting	—	52" x 76"

Making blocks

○ Create the blocks in the same way as for the table runner. You can stack and cut two, four, or six fabrics at a time. Make a total of 16 blocks. The quilt requires only 15 blocks, so you can use the extra one for a label.

○ Trim the blocks as instructed for the table runner, saving all the remainders for the borders and binding.

Quilt assembly

Quilt assembly

○ Sew the blocks together in rows of three across. Make five rows.

○ Sew the rows together. Sew and press carefully. The raw edges of the blocks are not on the straight of grain. The quilt measures 36½" x 60½".

Adding borders

Border 1:

○ Both borders are created from the remainders. Cut two 2¼" x 18" strips from each fat quarter remainder. Make two groups of strips that contain one of each fabric. One group is for the border, the other is for the binding.

○ Join four 2¼" strips, end to end, for each side border. Press the seam allowances open and trim the strips to 60½". Save the remainders.

○ Sew the pieced borders to the sides of the quilt and press the seam allowances toward the borders.

○ Join three 2¼" strips, end to end, for the top border and three for the bottom. Press allowances open. Trim the strips to 40". Add the two remaining strips to the binding group. Sew the borders to the top and bottom of the quilt.

Border 2:

- Square the short ends of all the pieced block remainders, taking off as little as possible. The remainders are about 14½" long. They do not need to be either specific or identical lengths. Trim to 4½" wide.

- For the top border, join three block remainders end to end. Press the seam allowances open and trim the strip to 40". Sew the strip to the top of the quilt. Repeat for the bottom border.

The side borders may need as much as 4" added to them to create the length needed. From the remainders that were trimmed from the inner border, cut 4½" segments and insert them into the pieced side borders as needed. Because the block remainders vary in length, your borders may require more than one insert.

- Join five block remainders with inserts for each side. Press seam allowances open

and trim to 72". Sew the strips to the quilt, which now measures 48" x 72".

Finishing

- Cut the backing yardage in half, selvage to selvage. Trim the selvages from the panels and sew the panels together along their length. Press.

- Layer the backing, batting, and quilt top and baste the layers.

- Quilt the layers. Use the reserved 2¼" strips to create a continuous binding strip 248" long.

The quilt in the photo below was quilted in the ditch on all block and border seams, both horizontally and vertically. Random curved quilting lines go up and across the quilt from border to border.

SEASON IN THE SERENGETI, by Cheryl Forsythe.

BENT PIECES, by the author.

Cutting Curves from Straight Pieces – Debbie Bowles

Follow Me

52" x 63½"
Sixteen 9½" x 12" blocks

You need a very sharp rotary cutter for this project. You must cut through five layers of pieced strips to make the color bands flow across the quilt. Although high contrast was used for the five color bands in the pictured quilt, imagine what it might look like if the five fabrics graduated from light to dark, all in the same color family.

FOLLOW ME, by the author.

Cutting Curves from Straight Pieces – Debbie Bowles

Fabric Requirements

Cut strips selvage to selvage.
These fabrics must have 42" useable width.

Fabrics	Yards	Cut
A, B, C, D, E	⅞ each	one 16" strip each two 4½" strips each
F (sashing)	⅜	four 2½" strips
Binding	½	or remainders, 2¼" strips
Backing	3¼	two 35" x 56" panels
Batting	—	56" x 67½"

Making Blocks

○ Organize the 16" A through E strips in the rotation of color you want to use.

Remember that the first and last fabrics will be adjacent to each other as the fabrics rotate. To see the bands of color flow across the quilt, similar colors should not be next to each other.

○ After cutting off selvages, *stack five strips right side up in the color rotation you have chosen.* Refer to the multiple cuts lesson to make four cuts, creating five sections.

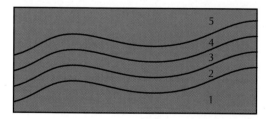

○ Arrange strips in sewing order, as follows:
Section 1: Leave as it is.
Section 2: Move top fabric to the bottom.
Section 3: Move top two fabrics to bottom.
Section 4: Move top three fabrics to bottom.
Section 5: Move bottom fabric to the top.

The top layer is one strip set. The second layer becomes the second strip set, and so on. For this project, sew together an entire strip set before moving to the next one. Organization is the key.

○ Make five strip sets. Do not trim the width. Carefully stack the five pieced strip sets in the same order they were stitched, matching the curved seams throughout the length of the strips. The outside edges will not align and will be trimmed later.

○ Trim only what is necessary to square the left edges of the strips because there is little extra on each strip. Cut four 10" segments from the stack.

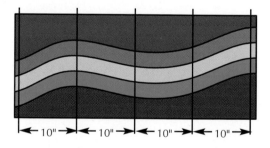

If you have a cutting surface that can accommodate the four stacks of segments, leave the blocks in place with the curves aligned, trim the width of each stack of blocks to 12½". Because the bands of color move across the quilt, the width of the blocks must be trimmed identically on all four stacks. If your cutting area isn't big enough, work on two groups at a time, take

Cutting Curves from Straight Pieces – Debbie Bowles

away the first group after trimming, slide the second stack over, and add the third stack, aligning the bands of color. Repeat the process until all stacks have been trimmed.

○ Trim the width of the sections to 12½", being careful that the curves still align across the strips.

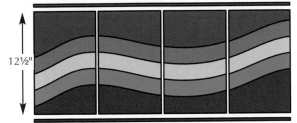

Quilt assembly

To create the quilt shown, use one block from each stack for a row. Look at the top left block of the photographed quilt. Purple is the bottom color. In the adjacent block, purple is the second color, then the third color, and it finishes as the fourth color. There will be four extra blocks. Save them for the sashing.

○ From the fabric F strips, cut twelve 12½" sashing strips, three per strip.

○ Sew the blocks and vertical sashing strips together in rows. Pin frequently to prevent distortion. Press toward the sashing. Rows measure 44½".

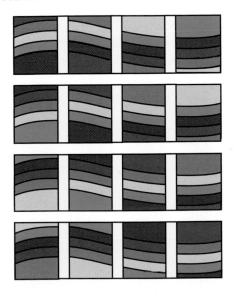

○ The four remaining blocks are cut and pieced to become the horizontal sashing. Cut each block into three 3" x 12½" segments. You will have twelve segments.

○ Sew four segments together to create each sashing piece. Trim to 44½". Make three. Press seam allowances in any direction.

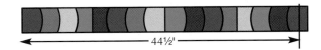

○ Sew the rows together. The quilt measures 44½" x 56". (Read below before stitching.)

The quilt in the photograph (page 69) has segments that have been rotated so that both the

Cutting Curves from Straight Pieces – Debbie Bowles

slant and the color vary. There are no seams to match when sewing the divider strips to the block and sashing rows, but the edges are not on the straight of grain, and they need to be handled and sewn carefully. Match the centers of the rows and pin generously before stitching. Remember, you are aligning the sashing strips from row to row when you sew. Press all seam allowances away from the horizontal sashing.

Adding borders

○ Sew the 4½" strips together in two groups of five. The fabrics can be in the same order you used before or in a different rotation. The seam allowances may be pressed in any direction.

○ Cut eleven 4½" segments from the strip sets. Save the remaining pieces of the strip sets for the binding.

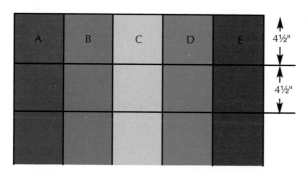

○ Unstitch one of the segments so you have five loose squares.

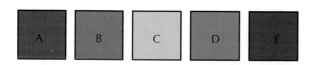

○ Referring to the photograph and quilt assembly diagram, place the segments around the quilt. The top and bottom borders require two segments plus one square. The sides each need three segments plus one square.

○ Sew segments and single squares together for the top and bottom borders, pressing seam allowances in any direction. The borders should measure 44½".

○ Sew the top and bottom borders to the quilt, pressing seam allowances toward the blocks.

○ Piece sixteen squares for each side. Correctly pieced, the sewn squares will measure 64½" in length, which is about ½" longer than the sides of the quilt top. Trimming equally from both ends, shorten the strips to 64".

○ Sew the strips to the sides of the quilt, pressing seam allowances toward the blocks. The quilt measures 52½" x 64".

Finishing

○ Cut the backing fabric in half, selvage to selvage, creating two panels. Trim off the selvages and sew the panels together on one long edge.

○ Layer the backing, batting, and quilt top and baste the layers.

○ Quilt the layers and bind the raw edges.

The quilt was first quilted in the ditch along all block, sashing, and divider seam lines. These quilting lines run from edge to edge, securing the borders. The curved seams were stitched in the ditch from edge to edge, including the borders. Your batting choice will determine if this is enough quilting for your project.

The binding was created from strip set remainders. Cut thirteen 2¼" segments from the set. Using straight seams, sew the segments to make one continuous strip 242".

Cutting Curves from Straight Pieces – Debbie Bowles

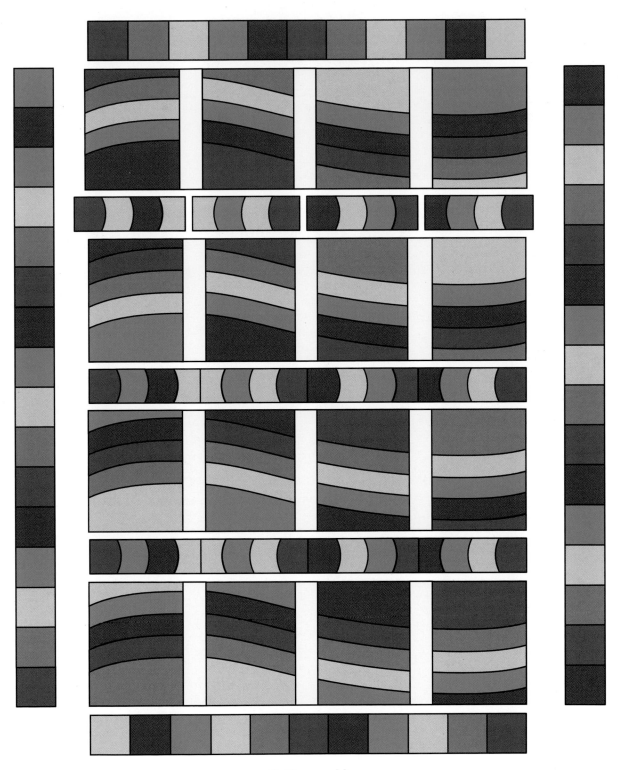

Quilt assembly

Cutting Curves from Straight Pieces – Debbie Bowles

Checkers

44" x 68"
Six 8" x 16" blocks

On the drawing board, this quilt top reminded me of the game of checkers with its circles and squares. I had intended to make it in reds, blacks, and whites. Somewhere along the way, the idea of pairs of blues and greens sidetracked me. What you see is three pairs of blue and green fabrics. The blue is the darker fabric in each pair. The lightest pair (A and B) are used in the circle blocks. The darkest pair (E and F) are in the pieced border. C and D are combined in the checkerboard squares in the quilt body. Perhaps you would like to try the red, white, and black color scheme.

CHECKERS, by the author; quilted by Brenda Leino.

Cutting Curves from Straight Pieces – Debbie Bowles

Fabric Requirements
Cut strips selvage to selvage.

Fabrics	Yards	First Cut	Second Cut
A (light)	¾	two 10" strips	six 10" squares
B (dark)	1⅝	two 10" strips	six 10" squares
border		ten 2½" strips	—
		one 6½" strip	four 6½" squares
C (light)	¾	four 4½" strips	—
D (dark)	¾	four 4½" strips	—
E (light)	½	four 2½" strips	—
F (dark)	½	four 2½" strips	—
Binding	½	six 2¼" strips	—
Backing	2⅞	two 37" x 48" panels	—
Batting	—	48" x 72"	—

Making blocks

○ Referring to the lesson on cutting arcs and half circles, layer a 10" A square and 10" B square, right sides up.

○ Fold the layered squares and place marks 2" up from the lower right corner and 5" down from the top left, on the fold. Draw the half arc and cut on the drawn line.

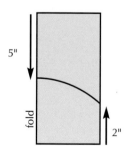

○ Unfold the layers. Place the sections in sewing order and sew together, clipping the curved allowances as needed. Press seam allowances toward the half circle.

○ Repeat these steps to create twelve half circles. Using the lesson on arcs and circles, trim the blocks to 8½" x 8½".

○ Sew together identical half circles to complete the circles. There will be three of each color combination. Press seam allowances in any direction. The completed circle blocks measure 8½" x 16½".

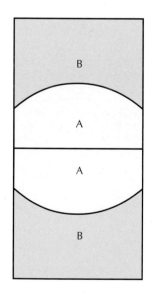 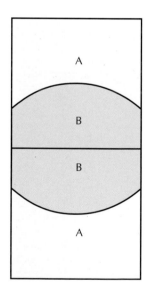

Sewing the checkerboard

○ Sew two C strips and two D strips together lengthwise, alternating fabrics. Press seam allowances toward D. Make two strip sets.

● Cut sixteen 4½" segments from strip sets.

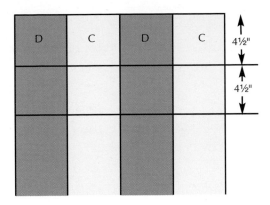

● Join two segments on one long side.

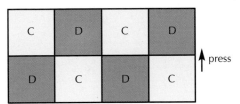

Make 4 for top and bottom rows.

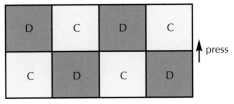

Make 2 for center row.

● Join two segments end to end. Make two. Press seam allowances toward D.

Quilt assembly

● Sew the circles and checkerboards together, pressing the seam allowances toward the circles.

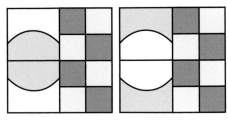

Top row

● Sew the pieces together by rows, then sew the rows together. Press seam allowances between rows in any direction.

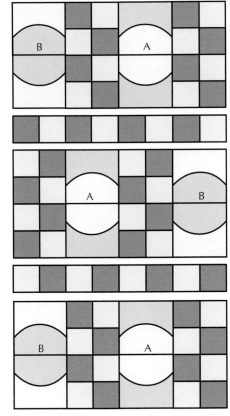

● Square the corners before adding borders. The quilt measures 32½" x 56½".

Adding borders

● Sew three 2½" B strips together end to end. Press seam allowances open and cut two 56½" lengths from the strip. Repeat to make a total of four 56½" lengths.

● Cut four 32½" segments of B.

● Join four E strips and four F strips, alternating fabrics. Press allowances toward F.

● Cut eleven 2½" segments from E/F strips.

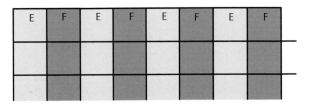

Cutting Curves from Straight Pieces – Debbie Bowles

○ The side borders each require 28 squares. Unstitch the middle seam of one eight-square E/F segment to make two four-square units.

○ Join three segments plus one four-square unit for each side.

○ Sew a 56½" B strip to both sides of the E/F strips. Press seam allowances toward B.

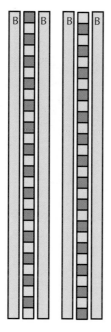

⬧ *Note that the upper-left side begins with an E square, and the upper-right side begins with an F. Press the seam allowances toward the border.*

○ Pin frequently and sew the pieced borders to the sides of quilt.

○ The top and bottom borders contain 16 squares each. Join two E/F segments, end to end, for the top border. Repeat for the bottom border.

○ Sew a B strip to both sides of the E/F sections. Press seam allowances toward B.

○ Sew a 6½" B square to both ends of each border. Press the seam allowances toward the centers of the strips.

The top border begins with an F square on the left, and the bottom begins with an E square.

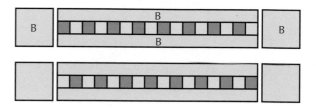

○ Pin frequently and sew the strips to the top and bottom.

○ Square the corners. The quilt measures 44½" x 68½".

Finishing

○ Cut the backing yardage in half, selvage to selvage. After removing the selvages, sew the two panels together on one long edge.

○ Layer the backing, batting, and quilt top and baste the layers.

○ Quilt the layers and bind the raw edges.

The quilt in the photo is quilted in an all-over meandering design that has pointy vines, curves, and star bursts.

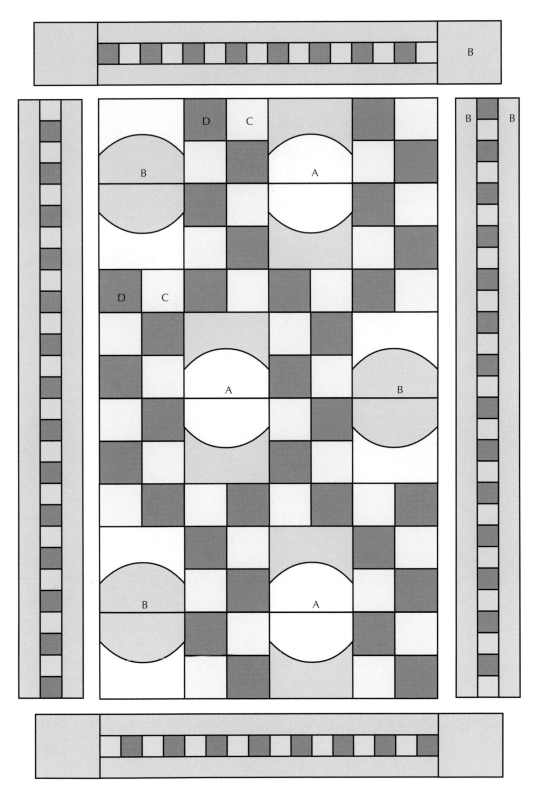

Quilt assembly

Cutting Curves from Straight Pieces – Debbie Bowles

Seeing You

40" x 40"
Sixteen 8" blocks

The pictured quilt shows two specialty fabrics at work, a directional print of dots in a curved line and a variegated fabric that moves from dark at both selvages to light in the center. This quilt shows what happens when you use a directional print for the circles.

The full circles in the quilt are made from pairs of half-circle blocks. If you use a directional print for the full circles, normally, you will want to rotate half the fabric squares 180 degrees before cutting the half-circle arcs. This rotation makes the print run in the same direction in both halves of the circle. However, for this quilt, I liked what was happening where the curves of the dots mirrored the shape of the half circle, so I did not rotate the fabrics squares, I stacked them identically.

The variegated fabric makes an easy, dramatic border because it darkens or lightens at the corners. Each strip is cut into two segments before cutting the curve, so there is automatically a dark end and a light end on each segment. As with all specialty fabrics, think and plan before cutting, then be happy with whatever fun effect emerges.

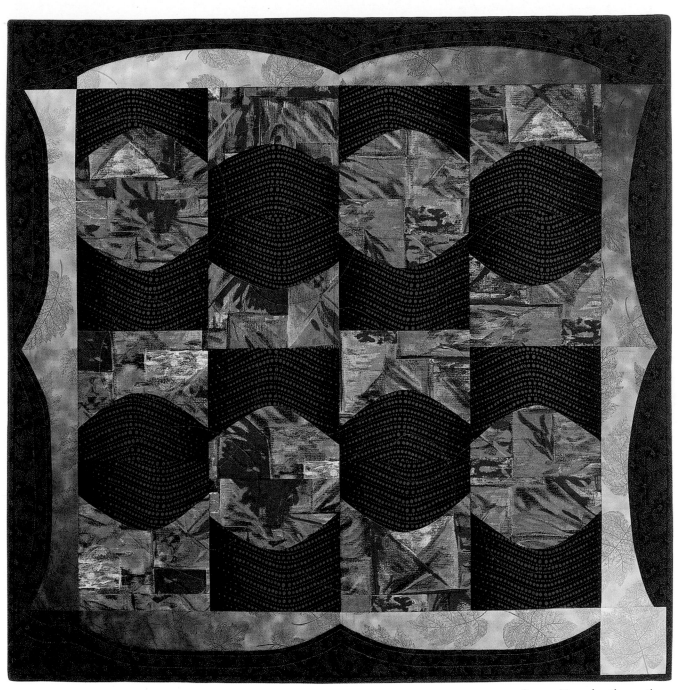

SEEING YOU, by the author.

Cutting Curves from Straight Pieces – Debbie Bowles

Fabric Requirements
Cut strips selvage to selvage.

Fabrics	Yards	First Cut	Second Cut
A & B	¾	two 10" strips each	eight 10" squares each
C	⅝	two 6" strips one 4½" strip	four 18" segments one 4½" square
D	⅝	two 6" strips one 4½" strip	four 18" segments three 4½" squares
Binding	⅜	five 2¼" strips	—
Backing	2⅝	two 24" x 44" panels	—
Batting	—	44" x 44"	—

Making blocks

○ Referring to the lesson on cutting arcs, layer a 10" A and 10" B square, right sides up.

○ Fold the layered squares in half, place marks 2" up from the lower right corner and 5" down from the top left, on the fold.

○ Draw the half arc and cut on the line.

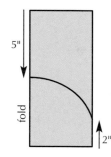

○ Unfold the layers. Place the sections in sewing order and sew them together, clipping the curved allowances as needed. Press toward the half circle.

○ Repeat these steps to create 16 half-circle blocks. Trim the blocks to 8½" x 8½".

○ Join identical half-circle blocks. Make eight, four of each kind. Press seam allowances in any direction. Full-circle blocks measure 8½" x 16½".

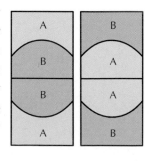

Quilt assembly

○ Using the quilt assembly diagram for placement, sew an A and a B circle block together, pinning to prevent stretching. Press seam allowances in any direction.

○ To prevent the circles from being identically aligned, two of the rows are shifted slightly by adding an extension. From a fabric A remainder or a 2" A strip, cut two 2" x 8½" segments.

○ Sew a 2" x 8½" A segment to the top of the rows beginning with a B circle. Press allowances in any direction. From the A circle side of the row, trim the rows to 16½".

○ Sew the four rows together, pressing all the seam allowances in the same direction. The quilt measures 32½" x 32½".

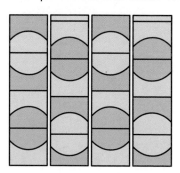

Cutting Curves from Straight Pieces – Debbie Bowles

Adding borders

◯ Refer to the lesson on cutting arcs. With right sides up, layer one 6" C and one 6" D strip.

◯ Fold the layered strips in half crosswise. Place a mark 1" up from lower-right corner and 3" down from upper-left, on the center fold. Draw and cut the half arc.

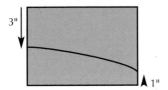

◯ Unfold layers and place sections in sewing order. Sew sections together, clipping curves. Make eight arc segments, four of each kind.

Before trimming the arc segments, try different arrangements for the arc borders. The options will change the look of the border and how you trim your segments.

◯ The ends of two arcs are joined to form a point in the middle. To achieve this sharp point, the two arcs that will be sewn together must be trimmed together. Layer the segments right sides together, aligning the curved seam lines before trimming.

◯ Trim the top edge 2" above the top of the arc, then trim the total width of the strip to 4½". Trimming equal amounts from both ends, shorten the length to 16½".

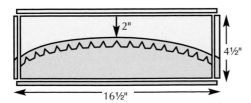

◯ Sew these two C arcs together end to end. Press seam allowances in any direction. Make two. Each border strip is 32½".

◯ Sew these border strips to the top and bottom of the quilt. Press seam allowances toward the border.

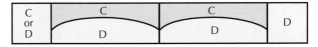

◯ Repeat trimming and stitching D arcs. Make two. The border measures 32½".

◯ Sew a 4½" C or D square to the ends of each border strip. (Only one of the squares is a C.) Press allowances toward the arcs.

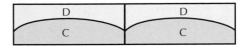

◯ Sew the borders to the sides of the quilt. Press seam allowances toward the borders.

◯ Square the corners and straighten the edges. The quilt measures 40½" x 40½".

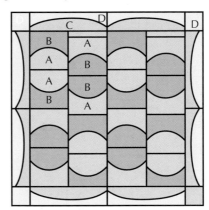

Finishing

◯ Cut the backing yardage in half, selvage to selvage. Trim selvages from the panels and sew them together on one long edge. Press.

◯ Layer the backing, batting, and quilt top and baste the layers. Quilt the layers and bind the raw edges.

In the photo, the blocks were quilted with a large loop-the-loop design. The quilting lines in the border echo the line of the arcs.

Cutting Curves from Straight Pieces – Debbie Bowles

Channel 32 2:00 a.m.

68" x 104"
Eighteen 12" blocks
Twin Size

This fun project provides a good way to use some of your fabric collection. Every fabric appears in two of the blocks. The arc fabrics (C and D) are both used as inside and outside sections of an arc. The cornerstones in each block match the center frame. To lessen the chance of confusing your fabrics, create only two blocks at a time, reversing the arc segments when assembling the block.

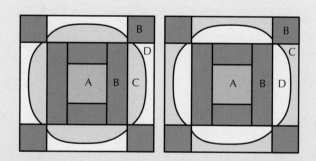

CHANNEL 32 – 2:00 A.M., by the author; quilting by Brenda Leino.

Cutting Curves from Straight Pieces – Debbie Bowles

Fabric Requirements

Cut strips selvage to selvage. Choose nine fabrics for each block location A, B, C, and D, for a total of thirty-six fabrics. Each group of four fabrics for the two blocks should have good contrast. *To avoid confusion, make only two blocks at a time.* In addition, cut one or two 4½" squares from all of the A, B, C, and D fabrics and the E border fabric to make a total of 54 squares for the pieced border.

Fabrics (whole quilt)	Yards (whole quilt)	First Cut (two blocks)	Second Cut (two blocks)
A (9 pieces)	⅜ each	one 4½" strip	two 4½" squares
B (9 pieces)	⅜ each	two 2½" strips	four 8½" segments
			four 4½" segments
			eight 2½" squares
C (9 pieces)	⅜ each	one 4" strip	four 10" segments
D (9 pieces)	⅜ each	one 4" strip	four 10" segments
E (border)	3½	twelve 2½" strips	—
		one 8½" strip	four 8½" squares
		nine 7½" strips	—
Accent border	½	eight 1½" strips	—
Binding	¾	nine 2¼" strips	—
		or remainders	
Backing	6⅜	two 37" x 108" panels	—
Batting	—	72" x 108"	—

Making blocks

○ Layer a C and a D segment right sides up, aligning the edges carefully.

○ Refer to the lesson on arcs, fold rectangles in half crosswise and place a mark 1½" up from the bottom right and 1" down from the top left. Draw the half arc and cut.

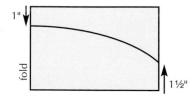

○ Place the arc sections in sewing order, then sew sections together. Clip the seam

allowances where necessary. Press all seam allowances toward the partial circle.

○ Trim the top edge ½" above the center of the arc, then trim the width to 2½".

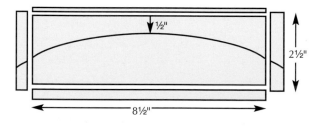

○ Taking equal amounts from each side, trim the pieces to 8½". Repeat with remaining C/D's and make eight.

Cutting Curves from Straight Pieces – Debbie Bowles

○ Following the block assembly diagrams, sew two blocks. Press seam allowances away from A. Square the blocks to 12½".

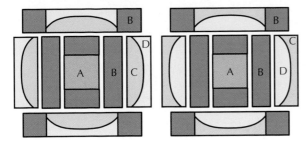

○ Use the previous instructions to make all nine pairs of blocks.

Quilt assembly

The blocks are arranged three across by six down. Sew the blocks in horizontal rows, then sew the rows together. The quilt measures 36½" x 72½". Square the corners and straighten the edges.

Adding borders

Border 1:

○ Look at the border construction in the quilt assembly diagram on page 88. For the top and bottom border-1 strips, make two sets of nine 4½" squares. Press all the seam allowances in the same direction. The sewn strips measure 36½" in length.

○ For the sides of the quilt, make two sets of eighteen 4½" squares. Press all the seam allowances in the same direction. These strips measure 72½" in length.

○ Sew a 72½" strips together end to end. Press the seam allowances open and trim the strips to 72½". Make four.

○ Sew a 72½" strip to each side of the strips with 18 squares, pinning often. Press seam allowances toward E. Make two of these border units.

○ Match the centers of the border units to the centers of the long quilt edges. Pin generously and stitch. Press seam allowances toward the borders.

○ Trim the four remaining 2½"-wide strips to 36½" long. Sew a 36½" strip to each side of the strips with nine squares, pinning frequently. Press seam allowances toward E. Make two of these border units.

○ Sew an 8½" square to each end of both border units and press seam allowances toward the center. Each border unit measures 52½".

○ Matching centers, pin the borders to the quilt and sew. Press seam allowances toward the borders. The quilt measures 52½" x 88½".

Border 2:

○ Sew three 1½" strips end to end and press the seam allowances open. Trim to 88½". Make two and save the remainders.

○ Sew the strips to the long sides of the quilt and press seam allowances outward.

○ Sew a remainder to another 1½" strip. Press seam allowances open and trim to 54½". Make two.

○ Sew these strips to the top and bottom of the quilt, which measures 54½" x 90½".

Border 3:

○ Sew three 7½" strips end to end. Press seam allowances open and cut two 54½" lengths from the sewn strips. Sew these to the top and bottom of the quilt. Press seam allowances outward.

○ Sew three more 7½" strips end to end. Press the seam allowances open and trim to 104½". Make two of these and sew them to the sides of the quilt. Press as before. The quilt measures 68½" x 104½".

○ The accent squares were sewn with a short, narrow zigzag stitch. These accents could also be fused or appliquéd. The quilt contains 22 randomly placed 4" and 4½" squares and one triangle. Try various arrangements to find one you like best.

Finishing

○ Cut the backing yardage in half, selvage to selvage, creating two panels. Sew them together on one long edge.

○ Layer the backing, batting, and quilt top and baste the layers. Quilt the layers and bind raw edges.

The blocks are quilted with large, random spirals done in variegated rayon thread. Borders have loop-the-loops in yellow rayon.

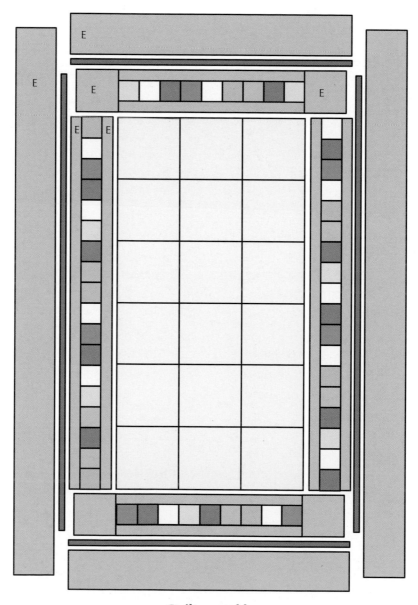

Quilt assembly

Cutting Curves from Straight Pieces – Debbie Bowles

CHANNEL 32 Wallhanging
40" x 40", Four 12" blocks

Fabric Requirements

Cut strips selvage to selvage.

Choose two fabrics for each block location A, B, C, and D, for a total of eight fabrics, ⅜ yard each. Each group of four fabrics for the blocks needs good contrast. For every two blocks, cut the A, B, C, and D strips, squares, and segments as listed for the twin-sized quilt on page 86. From the A, B, C, and D fabric remainders, cut 24 assorted 4½" squares for the pieced border.

Fabrics	Yards	Cut
Border E	1	eight 2½" x 24½" strips
		four 8½" squares
Binding	⅜	five 2¼" strips
		or remainders
Backing	2⅝	two 23" x 44" panels
Batting	—	44" x 44"

Quilt assembly

Make four blocks as shown in the twin-sized quilt project on page 86. Sew the blocks together, two across by two down.

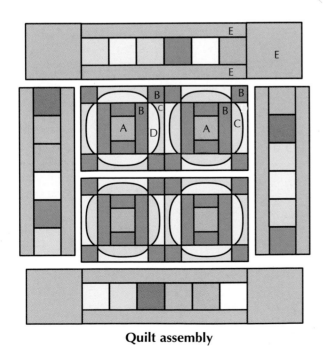

Quilt assembly

Adding borders

○ For the border strips, sew together six 4½" squares. Press all seam allowances in the same direction. Make four of these.

○ Sew a 24½" strip to both sides of each strip of squares. Press toward E.

○ Sew strips to two opposite sides of the quilt. Press seam allowances toward the border.

○ Sew an 8½" square to both ends of the two remaining strips. Press toward the center.

○ Sew these strips to the remaining sides of the quilt and press seam allowances toward the border. The quilt measures 40½" x 40½".

Finishing

Finish as described for the twin-sized quilt, on page 88.

Channel 32 Lap Size
44" x 80", Four 12" blocks

Fabric Requirements

Cut strips selvage to selvage.

Choose two fabrics for each block location A, B, C, and D, for a total of eight fabrics, ⅜ yard each. Each four block fabrics should have good contrast. For every two blocks, cut the A, B, C, and D strips, squares, and segments as listed for the twin-sized quilt on page 86. From the A, B, C, and D fabric remainders, cut 30 assorted 4½" squares for the pieced border.

Fabrics	Yards	Cut
Border 1 & 3	2¼	seven 2½" strips
		four 8½" squares
		six 7½" strips
Border 2	⅜	six 7½" strips
Binding	⅝	seven 2¼" strips
Backing	4¼	three 29" x 48" panels
Batting	—	48" x 84"

Quilt assembly

Make four circle blocks as shown in the twin-sized quilt instructions, page 86. Sew the blocks together in a row. The quilt measures 12½" x 48½".

Adding borders

Border 1:

❍ Sew 2½" strips together, end to end, to make the four 12½" lengths and the four 48½" lengths.

❍ Sew together two groups of three squares and two groups of twelve squares. Press all the seam allowances between the squares in the same direction.

❍ Sew the 48½" strips to the long sides of the strips with twelve squares to complete these border units.

❍ Match the centers of the border units to the centers of quilt edges. Pin generously and stitch to the quilt sides. Press the seam allowances toward the border.

❍ Sew a 12½" segment to both sides of border strips with three squares. Make two. Press seam allowances toward plain strip.

❍ Sew an 8½" square to each end of the remaining pieced strips. Press the seam allowances toward the center of the strip.

❍ Stitch these border units to the top and bottom of quilt. Press seam allowances toward the border. The quilt measures 28½" x 64½".

Border 2:

❍ Sew the 1½" border strips together end to end, as needed, to make two 64½" and two 30½" lengths.

❍ Sew long strips to the sides of the quilt and press seam allowances toward the border.

○ Sew a 30½" strip to the top and one to the bottom of the quilt. Press the seam allowances toward the border. The quilt now measures 30½" x 66½".

Border 3:

○ Sew the 7½" border strips together as needed to make the two 80½" lengths and the two 30½" lengths.

○ Sew 30½" lengths to top and bottom and 80½" lengths to the sides of the quilt. Press the seam allowances toward border. Quilt measures 44½" x 80½".

Finishing

Finish the quilt as described for the twin-sized quilt, page 88, except you will need three horizontal panels for the backing.

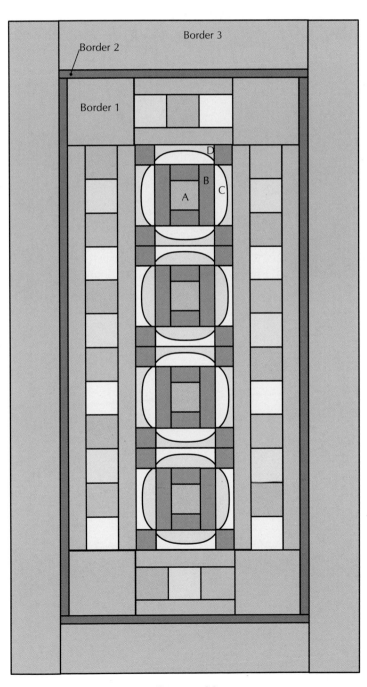

Quilt assembly

Cutting Curves from Straight Pieces – Debbie Bowles

Games

40" x 66"
Two 26" blocks

Two sizes of arcs were used to make this lap-sized quilt. You may recognize the inner 12" block from the quilt CHANNEL 32 – 2:00 A.M. on page 85. My sister thought this quilt looked like a board game from our childhood, Parcheesi, hence the name. Each 26" block has a different fabric for its outside edge. It would be easy to make a king-sized project with these large blocks.

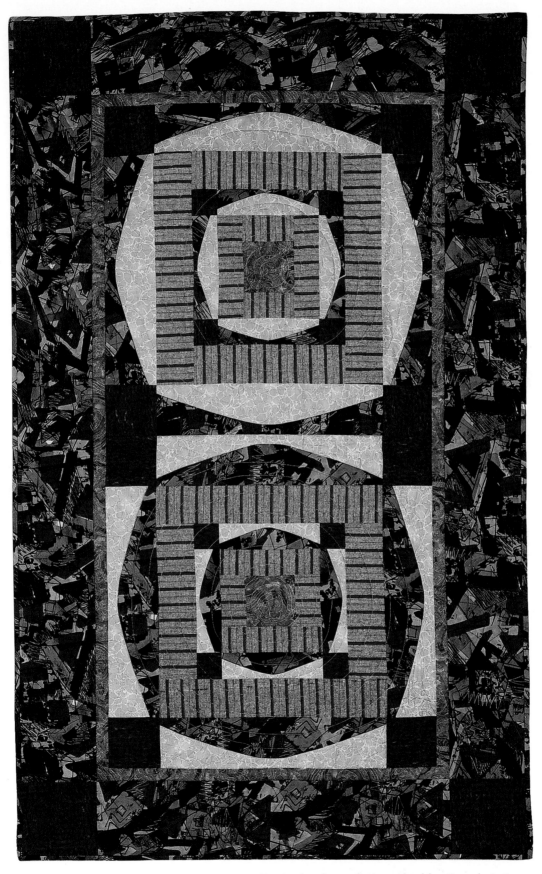

GAMES, by the author; quilted by Brenda Leino.

Cutting Curves from Straight Pieces – Debbie Bowles

Fabric Requirements
Cut strips selvage to selvage.

Fabrics	Yards	First Cut	Second Cut
A inner border	½	one 4½" strip five 1½" strips	two 4½" squares two 28½" strips
B	¾	two 2½" strips — four 3½" strips —	four 4½" segments four 8½" segments four 12½" segments four 18½" segments
C (light)	⅝	one 4" strip two 6" strips	four 10" segments four 20" segments
D (dark) border	1⅝	one 4" strip two 6" strips five 6½" strips	four 10" segments four 20" segments two 28½" segments
E border	½	one 2½" strip one 4½" strip one 6½" strip	eight 2½" squares eight 4½" squares four 6½" squares
Binding	½	six 2¼" strips	—
Backing	2¾	two 36" x 44" panels	—
Batting		44" x 70"	

Making small arcs

○ Refer to the lesson on cutting arcs. Layer a 4" x 10" C and a 4" x 10" D segment right sides up.

○ Fold the layered segments in half crosswise and place marks 1½" up from bottom-right corner and 1" down from top center, on the fold. Draw the half arc and cut on the line.

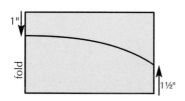

○ Unfold the layers. Place the sections in sewing order and sew them together, clipping the seam allowances as needed. Press seam allowances toward the half circle.

○ Repeat the steps to make eight arcs, four of each kind.

○ Trim top edge ½" from the top of the arc.

○ From bottom edge, trim total width to 2½".

○ Trimming equally from both sides, shorten the length to 8½".

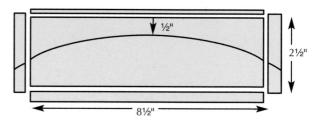

Making large arcs

○ Layer a 6" x 20" C and a 6" x 20" D segment right sides up.

○ Use small-arc instructions to make eight large arcs, four of each kind.

○ Trim the top edge ½" from the top of the the arc. From the bottom edge, trim the total width to 4½".

Cutting Curves from Straight Pieces – Debbie Bowles

- Trimming equally from both sides, shorten the length to 18½".

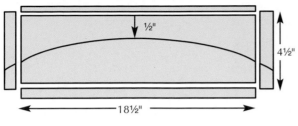

Block assembly

Keep C and D arcs in separate stacks and double check to be certain you are sewing the arcs in the correct orientation.

Following the block assembly diagrams, add segments to make one of each block. When adding the cornerstones, press seam allowances toward the arc. Press all other seam allowances outward.

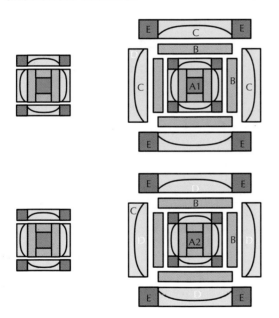

Quilt assembly

- Sew two blocks together and press the seam allowances in either direction. The quilt is 26½" x 52½".

- Sew three 1½" A strips end to end. From the pieced strip, cut two 52½" border strips and sew these to the sides of the quilt.

- Sew the 28½" A strips to the top and bottom of the quilt. The quilt is 28½" x 54½".

- Sew three 6½" D strips end to end. From the pieced strip, cut two 54½" border strips; sew to the sides.

- Sew a 6½" E square to both ends of the 28½" border strips. Press toward D.

- Sew the border strips to top and bottom of the quilt, which measures 40½" x 66½".

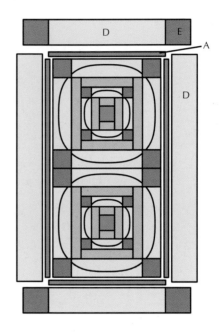

Quilt assembly

Finishing

- Cut backing yardage in half, selvage to selvage, creating two panels. Sew them together on one long edge. Press seam allowances open.

- Layer the backing, batting, and quilt top and baste the layers. Quilt the layers and bind the raw edges.

In the quilt on page 93, cornerstones have spiral quilting, while the main body is quilted with a large, irregularly spaced circles. The border was quilted with random straight lines.

Thelma's Choice

36" x 36"
Wallhanging

The THELMA'S CHOICE quilt is based on a traditional block of the same name. Although the two versions look quite different from each other, they are made from exactly the same pieced units. It's fun to be able to wait until the final border to decide what your project will look like. Notice that the cornerstones are cut from remainders. Although your squares will be similar, they will not be identical. The fabric requirements will make just one of these quilts.

A variation, shown on page 101, has a 12" (cut 12½") fabric square in the center in place of the nine patch, providing a good place for showing off that special fabric. Buy 1⅝ yards of B for Version 2.

Make several of these 36" blocks for an easy large quilt. For example, six blocks will make a quilt 72" x 108". The curved borders will form sashing where the blocks are joined. Where the cornerstones are joined, they will not create perfect points.

THELMA'S CHOICE, Version 1, by the author.

Cutting Curves from Straight Pieces – Debbie Bowles

Fabric Requirements
Cut strips selvage to selvage.

Fabrics	Yards	First Cut	Second Cut
A (light)	1⅜	four 8½" strips one 4½" strip two 2½" strips	four 27" strips four 4½" squares —
B (dark)	1⅜	four 8½" strips from 8½" remainders one 4½" strip two 2½" strips	four 27" segments eight 6½" squares five 4½" squares
Binding	⅜	four 2¼" strips	—
Backing	1¼	40" x 40"	—
Batting		40" x 40"	—

Cutting the arcs

O Refer to the lesson on cutting arcs. Layer an 8½" A and an 8½" B segment, right sides up.

O Fold the layered strips in half crosswise and place marks 1" up from the lower-right corner and 2½" down from the top left, on the fold.

O Draw the half arc and cut on the drawn line.

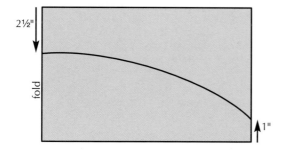

O Unfold the layers. Place the sections in sewing order and sew together, clipping the curved seam allowances. Press seam allowances toward the partial circle.

O Repeat the instructions to make eight arc sections, four of each kind.

O Working with one strip at a time, fold each strip in half crosswise and trim the top edge 1½" from the top of the arc.

O From the bottom of each strip, trim the total width to 6½".

O The A and B arcs are trimmed to different lengths. Trim the four B arcs to 24½", measure 12¼" from fold.

O Trim the four A arcs to 12½", measure 6¼" from fold. Save the remainders.

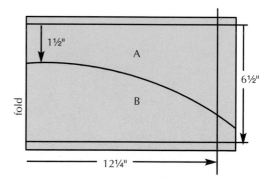

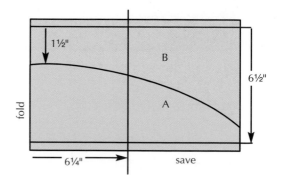

Cutting Curves from Straight Pieces – Debbie Bowles

○ Trim the four remainders to 6½" x 6½", leaving as much A showing as possible.

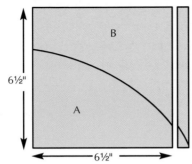

Adding angled ends

○ Mark a diagonal line, corner to corner, on the wrong side of the eight 6½" B squares.

○ With right sides together, place a square on top of each end of the 24½" B arcs, as shown in the figure. Stitch on the line.

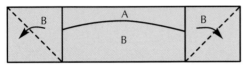

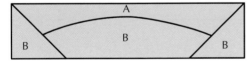

○ Fold each square in half along the seam line and press. Trim off the two bottom triangles, leaving a ¼" seam allowance. See the Sewing Tips for stars on page 55. Finished sections are 6½" x 24½".

Large nine patch

○ Using diagram below for placement, sew the 4½" squares in three rows of three, pressing the seam allowances toward B.

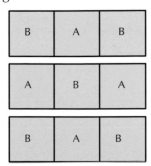

○ Sew the rows together, pressing the seam allowances in either direction. Make one nine patch and square it to 12½".

Small nine patches

○ Cut one of the 2½" A strips into two segments, one 25" and one 15". Repeat for one of the B strips.

○ Sew the remaining full-length A and B strips together on one long edge. Press the seam allowances toward B. Cut the sewn strip in two segments, one 25" and one 15".

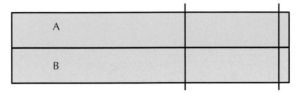

○ Using the 25" segments, make a B/A/B strip set and press toward B. Cut the strip set in eight 2½" segments.

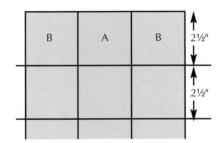

○ Using the 15" segments, make an A/B/A strip set and press the seam allowances toward B. Cut four 2½" segments from the strip set.

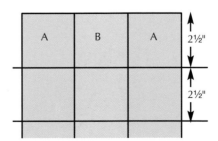

○ Sew three rows together to make a nine patch, pressing seam allowances in either direction. Make four nine patches and square to 6½".

Block assembly

○ Sew the 12½" A arcs to the sides of the large nine patch. Press the seam allowances outward.

○ Sew a 6½" nine patch to both ends of the remaining 12½" A arcs, pressing the seam allowances toward the arcs.

○ Sew these to the top and bottom of the nine patch. Press seam allowances outward. The block measures 24½" x 24½".

Decision time is now! The A edge faces out in Version 1. The B edge faces out in Version 2.

○ Sew the 24½" B arc to the sides, press the seam allowances outward.

○ Sew the 6½" square A/B segments to both ends of the remaining 24½" B arcs. Press seam allowances toward the arcs.

○ Sew these strips to the top and bottom of the block and press the seam allowances outward. The block measures 36½" x 36½".

○ Square the corners and straighten the edges. These edges are not on the straight of grain, so it's a good idea to staystitch around the perimeter of the quilt before proceeding with the quilting or binding.

Finishing

○ Layer the backing, batting, and quilt top and baste the layers. Quilt the layers and bind the raw edges.

The author quilted Version 1 by stitching in the ditch. She then simply followed the curve around with varying numbers of quilting lines. The center checkerboard has two diagonal lines. Version 2 was quilted by filling in much of the center with a vine type leaf.

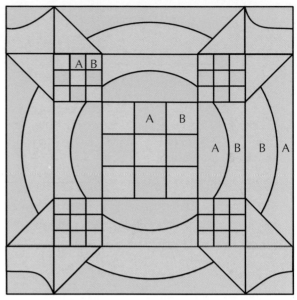

Version I

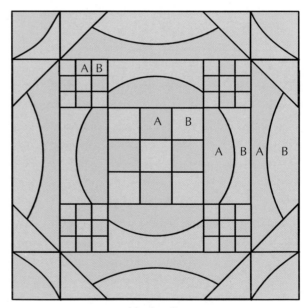

Version 2

Cutting Curves from Straight Pieces – Debbie Bowles

*THELMA'S CHOICE, Version 2, by the author;
quilted by Brenda Leino.*

THELMA'S CHOICE, by Beverly Dorsey, is a Version 2 variation.

Cutting Curves from Straight Pieces – Debbie Bowles

Royal Cross

42" x 42"
Eight 8" x 16" blocks
Two 16" x 16" blocks

ROYAL CROSS is based on a traditional block of the same name, and while it doesn't look exactly like its namesake, the feel of the block is similar. This quilt is a good example of using a traditional block for taking off in a new direction. The large corner triangles provide great places to show off a specialty fabric or fabulous quilting.

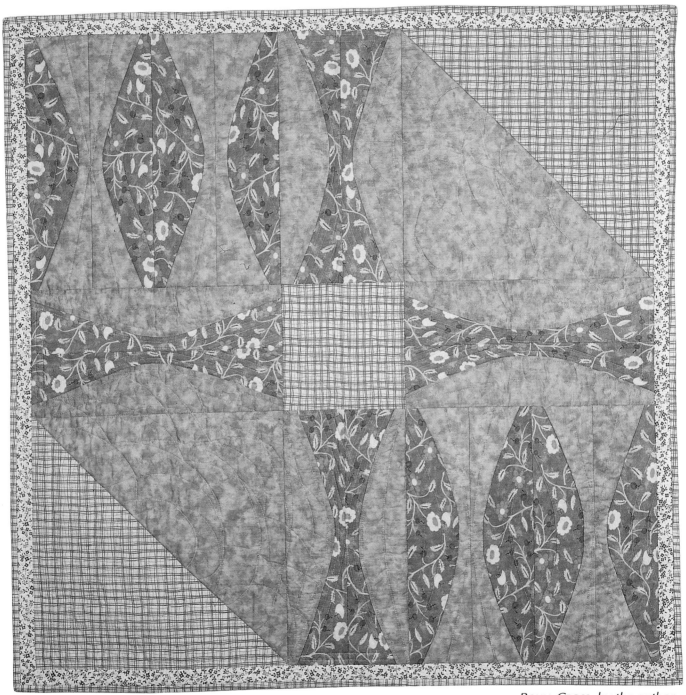

ROYAL CROSS, by the author.

Cutting Curves from Straight Pieces – Debbie Bowles

Fabric Requirements

Cut strips selvage to selvage.

Fabrics	Yards	First Cut	Second Cut
A	⅝	one 16⅞" strip	one 16⅞" square
		—	one 8½" square
B (dark)	⅞	four 6" strips	eight 18" segments
C (light)	1	one 18" strip	one 16⅞" square
		—	four 6" x 18" segments
		two 6" strips	four 18" segments
D (border)	⅜	five 1½" strips	—
Binding	½	five 2¼" strips	—
Backing	2¾	two 24" x 46" panels	—
Batting	—	46" x 46"	—

Sewing blocks

○ Refer to the lesson on cutting arcs, layer a 6" x 18" B, and a 6" x 18" C segment, right sides up.

○ Fold the layered strips in half crosswise. Place marks 1" up from the bottom right and 2" down from the top, on center fold.

○ Draw the half arc and cut on drawn line.

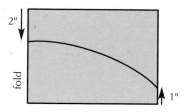

○ Unfold the layers. Place the sections in sewing order and sew them together, clipping the curved seam allowances as needed. Press seam seam allowances toward the partial circle. Repeat these steps to create sixteen arc segments.

○ Trim the top edge of each segment 1" from the top center of the arc. From the bottom edge, trim the width to 4½".

○ Taking equal amounts from both sides, trim the length of the arc to 16½".

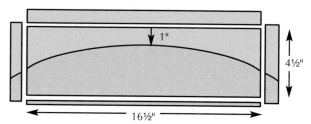

○ Sew pairs of arcs together as shown below. Make four of each type of block, pinning the edges to prevent stretching. Press seam allowances in either direction.

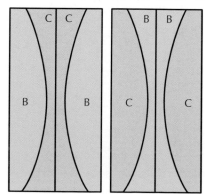

Half-square blocks

○ With right sides together, layer the two 16⅞" squares, cut them diagonally, corner to corner, and sew the pairs of triangles

Cutting Curves from Straight Pieces – Debbie Bowles

together on their long edges. Press seam allowances in either direction. Trim the half squares to 16½" x 16½".

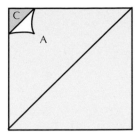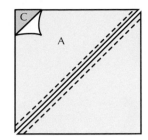

Quilt assembly

○ Position the blocks and half squares according to the illustration below. Pinning all seams to prevent stretching, sew pieces together by rows. Press seam allowances as shown by arrows.

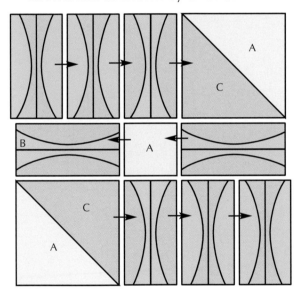

○ Join rows, pinning and matching seams. Square the corners and straighten the edges. The quilt measures 40½" x 40½".

Adding borders

○ Cut two of the D border strips to 40½". Pinning generously, sew these strips to the sides of the quilt and press the seam allowances toward the border.

○ Sew the three remaining border strips together, end to end. Press the seam allowances open and cut two 42½" lengths from the pieced strip.

○ Pin generously and sew the strips to the top and bottom of the quilt. Press the seam allowances toward the border. The quilt measures 42½" x 42½".

Finishing

○ Cut the backing yardage in half, selvage to selvage, creating two panels. Remove the selvages and sew the panels together along one long edge. Press the seam allowances open.

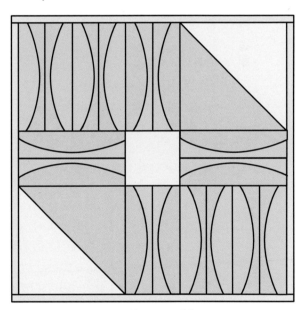

Quilt assembly

○ Layer the backing, batting, and quilt top and baste the layers. Quilt the layers and bind the raw edges.

The large yellow corner triangles are quilted in L-shaped lines, and the lavender portions in a shell pattern. The quilting lines in the rest of the quilt echo the arcs.

Cutting Curves from Straight Pieces – Debbie Bowles

Royal Circles

80" x 104"
Thirty-four 8" x 16" blocks

Fabric A has a chance to shine in this quilt. If you love to highlight your quilting skills, these large 16" squares provide a wonderful place to do so.

Directional fabrics are not recommended for A or B. The A fabric in the quilt on the facing page is almost a stripe. It is one of those trick fabrics in which the pattern is more distinct after being cut than it was while on the bolt. The dark smudges definitely form a line in the large square. Notice that, on the border arcs, the smudges do not line up. If fabric surprises, like these smudges, don't appeal to you, avoid using directional and stripe-like fabrics for arc segments.

ROYAL CROSS, by the author; quilted by Brenda Leino.

Cutting Curves from Straight Pieces – Debbie Bowles

Fabric Requirements
Cut strips selvage to selvage.

Fabrics	Yards	First Cut	Second Cut
A (light)	4¾	seventeen 6" strips	thirty-four 18" segments
		three 16½" strips	six 16½" squares
		one 8½" strip	four 8½" squares
B (dark)	4¾	seventeen 6" strips	thirty-four 18" segments
		eighteen 2½" strips	—
		two 1½" strips	eight 8½" segments
		one 6½" strip	four 8½" segments
C	⅞	three 8½" strips	twelve 8½" squares
Binding	⅞	ten 2¼ strips	—
Backing	7½	three 36" x 84" panels	—
Batting		84" x 108"	—

Making blocks

○ Referring to the lesson on cutting arcs, layer a 6" x 18" A and a 6" x 18" B segment, right sides up.

○ Fold layered strips in half crosswise. Place marks 1" up from the bottom right and 2" down from the top, on the center fold.

○ Draw the half arc and cut on the line.

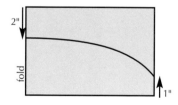

○ Unfold the layers. Place the sections in sewing order and sew them together, clipping the curved seam allowances as needed. Press seam allowances toward the partial circle. Repeat the steps to create 68 arc segments, 34 of each.

○ Trim the top edge of each segment 1" from the top center of the arc. From the bottom edge, trim the width to 4½".

○ Taking equal amounts from both sides, trim the length of the arcs to 16½"

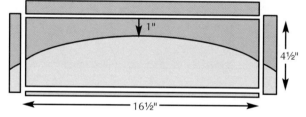

○ The arc segments are joined on the long side, with the curve toward the inside seam. Make 17 of each type of block, pinning the edges generously to prevent distortion. Press seam allowances in either direction. Trim to 8½" x 16½".

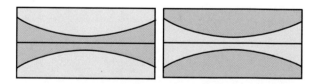

Quilt assembly

○ Position the blocks and squares as shown in the quilt assembly diagram. Pinning frequently, sew the blocks and squares in rows. Press seam allowances of pieced blocks toward unpieced squares. All rows measure 56½".

Cutting Curves from Straight Pieces – Debbie Bowles

○ Join the rows, pinning frequently and aligning block seams. Press the seam allowances between rows in either direction. The quilt measures 56½" x 80½".

Adding borders

Border 1:

○ Sew together three 2½" B strips, end to end, and cut two 56½" lengths from the pieced strip. Sew the strips to the top and bottom of the quilt. Press toward the border.

○ Sew together five 2½" B strips and cut two 84½" lengths. Sew the strips to the sides of the quilt. Press toward the border. The quilt measures 60½" x 84½". Square the corners and straighten the edges.

Border 2:

After piecing this border, there will be one extra segment. Consider using it for a label.

○ Beginning and ending with arc segments, alternate four 1½" x 8½" B segments with five arc segments. Press toward the B segments. Make two. Borders measure 84½".

○ Stitch the pieced borders to the sides of the quilt. Press toward the border.

○ Beginning and ending with arc segments, alternate two 6½" x 8½" B segments with three arc segments. Press away from the arc segments. Make two.

○ Sew 8½" A squares to both ends of each pieced border strip. Press toward the arc segments. The borders measure 76½".

○ Sew the pieced borders to the top and bottom of the quilt. Press toward the border. The quilt measures 76½" x 100½". Square the corners and straighten the edges.

Border 3:

○ Sew together two 2½" B strips, end to end, and cut a 76½" length. Make 2. Sew the border strips to the top and bottom of the quilt. Press toward the border.

○ Sew together three 2½" B strips, end to end, and cut a 104½" length. Make 2. Sew the border strips to the sides. Press toward the border. The quilt is 80½" x 104½".

Finishing

○ Cut the backing yardage in thirds, selvage to selvage, creating three equal panels. Remove the selvages and sew the panels together on their long edges. Press the seam allowances open.

○ Layer the backing, batting, and quilt top and baste the layers. Quilt the layers and bind the raw edges.

Quilt assembly

Cutting Curves from Straight Pieces – Debbie Bowles

Resources

Maple Island Quilts
Debbie Bowles, owner
329 Maple Island Road
Burnsville, MN 55306
E-mail: dbowles@mediaone.net
*Debbie is available for teaching and
lecturing engagements.*

Marbled Fabric and Accessories
Marjorie Lee Behvis, owner
Phone: 707-762-7514
Fax: 707-762-2548
E-mail: marjorie@marbled fabrics.com
www.marbledfabrics.com

About the Author

Debbie came to quiltmaking via a lifetime of garment and craft sewing and from a family of "makers" – everything from beautiful handstitched quilts from Grandma T to a personal favorite, table decorations made from furnace filters!

As an elementary school teacher, Cub Scout den mom, and church worker with junior high students, Debbie's approach to design, quiltmaking, and teaching means having fun while creating something that pleases you.

Debbie credits the many quiltmakers who came earlier with tools and methods that not only speeded the process of quiltmaking but also opened the doors for slightly non-traditional techniques to be accepted and enjoyed.

Through her pattern company, Maple Island Quilts, Debbie brings achievable and low-frustration techniques and designs to quilters of many skill levels. As quilting has become global, she cherishes the opportunities to teach, lecture, and talk fabric with quilters from all parts of the world.

Debbie lives in Burnsville, Minnesota, with her husband, Rick, and teenage sons, Ryan and Kyle.

OTHER AQS BOOKS

AQS books are known worldwide for timely topics, clear writing, beautiful color photos, and accurate illustrations and patterns. This is only a small selection of the books available from your local bookseller, quilt shop or public library.

#5753   U.S. $19.95

#5759   U.S. $19.95

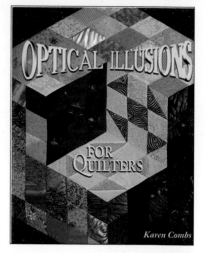

#4831   U.S. $22.95

#5756   U.S. $19.95

#3468   U.S. $34.95

#4957 (HB)   U.S. $34.95

#5710   U.S. $19.95

#5211   U.S. $18.95

#4697   U.S. $24.95

Look for these books nationally or call **1-800-626-5420**